W9-BZA-510

PARADISE
AND POWER

ALSO BY ROBERT KAGAN

A Twilight Struggle:
American Power and Nicaragua, 1977–1990

Present Dangers: Crisis and Opportunity in American
Foreign and Defense Policy (edited with William Kristol)

PARADISE AND POWER

*America and Europe
in the New World Order*

ROBERT KAGAN

Atlantic Books
London

First published in the United States of America in 2003 by Alfred A. Knopf

First published in Great Britain in 2003 by Atlantic Books,
an imprint of Grove Atlantic Ltd

Copyright © Robert Kagan 2003

The moral right of Robert Kagan to be identified as the author of this work
has been asserted in accordance with the Copyright, Designs and Patents
Act of 1988.

All rights reserved. No part of this publication may be reproduced, stored in a
retrieval system, or transmitted in any form or by any means, electronic,
mechanical, photocopying, recording, or otherwise, without the prior
permission of both the copyright owner and the above publisher of this book.

A shorter version of this essay originally appeared as an article entitled
'Power and Weakness' in *Policy Review* (June/July 2002).

3 5 7 9 10 8 6 4

A CIP catalogue record for this book is available from the British Library.

ISBN 1 84354 177 7

Printed in Great Britain by CPD Wales

Atlantic Books
An imprint of Grove Atlantic Ltd
Ormond House
26–27 Boswell Street
London WC1N 3JZ

For Leni and David

PARADISE
AND POWER

IT IS TIME to stop pretending that Europeans and Americans share a common view of the world, or even that they occupy the same world. On the all-important question of power—the efficacy of power, the morality of power, the desirability of power—American and European perspectives are diverging. Europe is turning away from power, or to put it a little differently, it is moving beyond power into a self-contained world of laws and rules and transnational negotiation and cooperation. It is entering a post-historical paradise of peace and relative prosperity, the realization of Immanuel Kant's "perpetual peace." Meanwhile, the United States remains mired in history, exercising power in an anarchic Hobbesian world where international laws and rules are unreliable, and where true security and the defense and promotion of a liberal order still depend on the possession and use of military might. That is why on major strategic and international questions today, Americans are from Mars and Europeans are from Venus: They agree on little and understand one another less and less. And this state of affairs is not transitory—the product of one American election or one catastrophic event. The reasons for the transatlantic divide are deep, long in development, and likely to endure. When it comes to setting national priorities, determining threats, defining challenges, and fashioning and implementing foreign and defense policies, the United States and Europe have parted ways.

It is easier to see the contrast as an American living in Europe. Europeans are more conscious of the growing differences, perhaps because they fear them more. European intellectuals are nearly unanimous in the conviction that Americans and Europeans no longer share a common "strategic culture." The European caricature at its most extreme depicts an America dominated by a "culture of death," its warlike temperament the natural product of a violent society where every man has a gun and the death penalty reigns. But even those who do not make this crude link agree there are profound differences in the way the United States and Europe conduct foreign policy.

The United States, they argue, resorts to force more quickly and, compared with Europe, is less patient with diplomacy. Americans generally see the world divided between good and evil, between friends and enemies, while Europeans see a more complex picture. When confronting real or potential adversaries, Americans generally favor policies of coercion rather than persuasion, emphasizing punitive sanctions over inducements to better behavior, the stick over the carrot. Americans tend to seek finality in international affairs: They want problems solved, threats eliminated. And, of course, Americans increasingly tend toward unilateralism in international affairs. They are less inclined to act through international institutions

such as the United Nations, less likely to work coopera-
tively with other nations to pursue common goals, more
skeptical about international law, and more willing to
operate outside its strictures when they deem it necessary,
or even merely useful.[1]

Europeans insist they approach problems with greater
nuance and sophistication. They try to influence others
through subtlety and indirection. They are more tolerant of failure, more patient when solutions don't come
quickly. They generally favor peaceful responses to problems, preferring negotiation, diplomacy, and persuasion
to coercion. They are quicker to appeal to international
law, international conventions, and international opinion
to adjudicate disputes. They try to use commercial and
economic ties to bind nations together. They often emphasize process over result, believing that ultimately process
can become substance.

This European portrait is a dual caricature, of course,
with its share of exaggerations and oversimplifications.
One cannot generalize about Europeans: Britons may
have a more "American" view of power than many Europeans on the Continent. Their memory of empire, the
"special relationship" with the United States forged in
World War II and at the dawn of the Cold War, and their
historically aloof position with regard to the rest of Europe tend to set them apart. Nor can one simply lump

[1] One representative French observer describes "a U.S. mindset"
that "tends to emphasize military, technical and unilateral solutions to
international problems, possibly at the expense of co-operative and
political ones." See Gilles Andreani, "The Disarray of U.S. Non-
Proliferation Policy," *Survival* 41 (Winter 1999–2000): 42–61.

French and Germans together: the first proud and independent but also surprisingly insecure, the second mingling self-confidence with self-doubt since the end of the Second World War. Meanwhile, the nations of Eastern and Central Europe have an entirely different history from their Western European neighbors, a historically rooted fear of Russian power and consequently a more American view of the Hobbesian realities. And, of course, there are differing perspectives within nations on both sides of the Atlantic. French Gaullists are not the same as French Socialists. In the United States, Democrats often seem more "European" than Republicans; Secretary of State Colin Powell may appear more "European" than Secretary of Defense Donald Rumsfeld. Many Americans, especially among the intellectual elite, are as uncomfortable with the "hard" quality of American foreign policy as any European; and some Europeans value power as much as any American.

Nevertheless, the caricatures do capture an essential truth: The United States and Europe are fundamentally different today. Powell and Rumsfeld have more in common than do Powell and the foreign ministers of France, Germany, or even Great Britain. When it comes to the use of force, most mainstream American Democrats have more in common with Republicans than they do with most Europeans. During the 1990s even American liberals were more willing to resort to force and were more Manichean in their perception of the world than most of their European counterparts. The Clinton administration bombed Iraq as well as Afghanistan and Sudan. Most European governments, it is safe to say, would not have done so and were, indeed, appalled at American militarism. Whether Europeans even would have bombed Belgrade in 1999 had the United States not forced their hand is an interesting question.[2] This past October, a majority of Senate Democrats supported the resolution authorizing President Bush to go to war with Iraq, while their political counterparts in France, Germany, Italy, Belgium, and even the United Kingdom looked on in amazement and some horror.

What is the source of these differing strategic perspectives? The question has received too little attention in recent years. Foreign policy intellectuals and policymakers on both sides of the Atlantic have denied the existence of genuine differences or sought to make light of present disagreements, noting that the transatlantic alliance has had moments of tension in the past. Those who have taken the present differences more seriously, especially in Europe, have been more interested in assailing the United States than in understanding why the United States acts as it does—or, for that matter, why Europe acts as it does. It is past time to move beyond the denial and the insults and to face the problem head-on.

Despite what many Europeans and some Americans believe, these differences in strategic culture do not

[2] The case of Bosnia in the early 1990s stands out as an instance where some Europeans, chiefly British Prime Minister Tony Blair, were at times more forceful in advocating military action than first the Bush and then the Clinton administration. (Blair was also an early advocate of using air power and even ground troops in the Kosovo crisis.) And Europeans had forces on the ground in Bosnia when the United States did not, although in a UN peacekeeping role that proved ineffective when challenged.

spring naturally from the national characters of Americans and Europeans. What Europeans now consider their more peaceful strategic culture is, historically speaking, quite new. It represents an evolution away from the very different strategic culture that dominated Europe for hundreds of years—at least until World War I. The European governments—and peoples—who enthusiastically launched themselves into that continental war believed in *Machtpolitik*. They were fervent nationalists who had been willing to promote the national idea through force of arms, as the Germans had under Bismarck, or to promote *egalité* and *fraternité* with the sword, as Napoleon had attempted earlier in the century, or to spread the blessings of liberal civilization through the cannon's mouth, as the British had throughout the seventeenth, eighteenth, and nineteenth centuries. The European order that came into being with the unification of Germany in 1871 was, "like all its predecessors, created by war."[3] While the roots of the present European worldview, like the roots of the European Union itself, can be traced back to the Enlightenment, Europe's great-power politics for the past three hundred years did not follow the visionary designs of the philosophes and the Physiocrats.

As for the United States, there is nothing timeless about the present heavy reliance on force as a tool of international relations, nor about the tilt toward unilateralism and away from a devotion to international law. Americans are children of the Enlightenment, too, and in the early

[3] Michael Howard, *The Invention of Peace* (New Haven, 2001), p. 47.

years of the republic were more faithful apostles of its creed. At its birth America was the great hope of Enlightenment Europeans, who despaired of their own continent and viewed America as the one place "where reason and humanity" might "develop more rapidly than anywhere else."[4] The rhetoric, if not always the practice, of early American foreign policy was suffused with the principles of the Enlightenment. American statesmen of the late eighteenth century, like the European statesmen of today, extolled the virtues of commerce as the soothing balm of international strife and appealed to international law and international opinion over brute force. The young United States wielded power against weaker peoples on the North American continent, but when it came to dealing with the European giants, it claimed to abjure power and assailed as atavistic the power politics of the eighteenth- and nineteenth-century European empires.

Some historians have gleaned from this the mistaken view that the American founding generation was utopian, that it genuinely considered power politics "alien and repulsive" and was simply unable to "comprehend the importance of the power factor in foreign relations." [5] But George Washington, Alexander Hamilton, John Adams, and even Thomas Jefferson were not utopians. They were well versed in the realities of international power politics. They could play by European rules when circumstances permitted and often wished they had the power to play the

[4] Robert R. Palmer, *The Age of the Democratic Revolution: A Political History of Europe and America, 1760–1800* (Princeton, 1959), 1:242.

[5] Felix Gilbert, *To the Farewell Address: Ideas of Early American Foreign Policy* (Princeton, 1961), p. 17.

game of power politics more effectively. But they were realistic enough to know that they were weak, and both consciously and unconsciously they used the strategies of the weak to try to get their way in the world. They denigrated power politics and claimed an aversion to war and military power, all realms in which they were far inferior to the European great powers. They extolled the virtues and ameliorating effects of commerce, where Americans competed on a more equal plane. They appealed to international law as the best means of regulating the behavior of nations, knowing well they had few other means of constraining Great Britain and France. They knew from their reading of Vattel that in international law, "strength or weakness . . . counts for nothing. A dwarf is as much a man as a giant is; a small Republic is no less a sovereign State than the most powerful Kingdom."[6] Later generations of Americans, possessed of a great deal more power and influence on the world stage, would not always be as enamored of this constraining egalitarian quality of international law. In the eighteenth and early nineteenth centuries, it was the great European powers that did not always want to be constrained.

Two centuries later, Americans and Europeans have traded places—and perspectives. This is partly because in those two hundred years, and especially in recent decades, the power equation has shifted dramatically: When the United States was weak, it practiced the strategies of indirection, the strategies of weakness; now that the United

[6] Quoted in Gerald Stourzh, *Alexander Hamilton and the Idea of Republican Government* (Stanford, 1970), p. 134.

States is powerful, it behaves as powerful nations do. When the European great powers were strong, they believed in strength and martial glory. Now they see the world through the eyes of weaker powers. These very different points of view have naturally produced differing strategic judgments, differing assessments of threats and of the proper means of addressing them, different calculations of interest, and differing perspectives on the value and meaning of international law and international institutions.

But even the power gap offers only part of the explanation for the broad gulf that has opened between the United States and Europe. For along with these natural consequences of the transatlantic disparity of power, there has also opened a broad ideological gap. Europeans, because of their unique historical experience of the past century—culminating in the creation of the European Union—have developed a set of ideals and principles regarding the utility and morality of power different from the ideals and principles of Americans, who have not shared that experience. If the strategic chasm between the United States and Europe appears greater than ever today, and grows still wider at a worrying pace, it is because these material and ideological differences reinforce one another. The divisive trend they together produce may be impossible to reverse.

THE POWER GAP

Some might ask, what is new? It is true that Europe has been declining as a global military power for a long time. The most damaging blow to both European power and confidence fell almost a century ago, in the world war that broke out in 1914. That horrendous conflict devastated three of the five European powers—Germany, Austria-Hungary, and Russia—that had been key pillars of the continental balance of power since 1871. It damaged European economies, forcing them into decades-long dependence on American bankers. But most of all, the war destroyed the will and spirit of Great Britain and France, at least until the British rallied under Churchill in 1939, when it was too late to avoid another world war. In the 1920s, Britain reeled from the "senseless" slaughter of a whole generation of young men at Passchendaele and other killing fields, and the British government began at war's end the rapid demobilization of its army. A frightened France had struggled to maintain adequate military force to deter what it considered the inevitable return of German power and revanchism. In the early 1920s, France was desperate for an alliance with Great Britain, but the Anglo-American guarantee to defend France stipulated in the Versailles Treaty vanished into thin air when the U.S. Senate refused to ratify it. Meanwhile, the traumatized British, somehow convincing themselves against all reason that France, not Germany, was the greatest threat to European peace, proceeded to insist, as late as 1934, that France disarm itself to the level of Germany. Winston Churchill's was a lonely voice warning of the "awful danger" of "perpetually asking the French to weaken themselves."[7]

The interwar era was Europe's first attempt to move beyond power politics, to make a virtue out of weakness. Instead of relying on power, as they had in the past, the European victors in World War I put their faith in "collective security" and in its institutional embodiment, the League of Nations. "Our purpose," declared one of the league's leading statesmen, was "to make war impossible, to kill it, to annihilate it. To do this we had to create a system."[8] But the "system" did not work, in part because its leading members had neither the power nor the will. It is ironic that the driving intellectual force behind this effort to solve Europe's security crisis through the creation of a supranational legal institution was an American, Woodrow Wilson. Wilson spoke with the authority of what had in recent decades become one of the world's richest and most powerful countries, and whose late entry into World War I had significantly aided the Allied victory. Unfortunately, Wilson spoke for America at a time when it, too, was running away from power, and, as it turned out, he did not actually speak for his country. The American refusal to participate in the institution Wilson created destroyed whatever small chance it may have had to succeed. As Churchill wryly recalled, "We, who had deferred so much to [Wilson's] opinions and wishes in all this busi-

[7] Winston Churchill, *The Gathering Storm* (Boston, 1948), p. 94.

[8] Edvard Benes quoted in E. H. Carr, *The Twenty Years' Crisis, 1919–1939* (London, 1948), p. 30.

ness of peacemaking, were told without much ceremony that we ought to be better informed about the American Constitution."9 The Europeans were left to themselves, and when confronted by the rising power of a rearming, revisionist Germany in the 1930s, "collective security" melted away and was replaced by the policy of appeasement.

At its core, the appeasement of Nazi Germany was a strategy based on weakness, which derived less from genuine inability to contain German power than from the understandable fear of another great European war. But built on top of this foundation was an elaborate structure of sophisticated arguments about the nature of the threat posed by Germany and the best means of addressing it. British officials, in particular, consistently downplayed the threat, or insisted that it was not yet serious enough to require action. "If it could be proved that Germany was rearming," the British Conservative leader Stanley Baldwin said in 1933, then Europe would have to do something. "But that situation had not yet arisen."10 Proponents of appeasement produced many reasons why the application of power was unnecessary or inappropriate. Some argued that Germany and its Nazi government had legitimate grievances that had to be taken into account by the Western powers. The Versailles Treaty, as John Maynard Keynes explained, had been harsh and counterproductive, and Britain and France had only themselves to blame if Ger-

9 Churchill, *The Gathering Storm*, p. 12.
10 Quoted in A. J. P. Taylor, *The Origins of the Second World War* (New York, 1983), pp. 73–74.

man politics had turned angry and revanchist. When Hitler complained about the mistreatment of ethnic Germans in Czechoslovakia and elsewhere, the Western democracies were prepared to concede the point. Nor did the other European powers want to believe that an ideological rift made compromise with Hitler and the Nazis impossible. In 1936 the French prime minister, Léon Blum, told a visiting German minister, "I am a Marxist and a Jew," but "we cannot achieve anything if we treat ideological barriers as insurmountable."[11] Many convinced themselves that although Hitler seemed bad, the alternatives to him in Germany were probably worse. British and French officials worked to gain Hitler's signature on agreements, believing he alone could control what were assumed to be the more extreme forces in German society.[12]

The purpose of appeasement was to buy time and hope that Hitler could be satisfied. But the strategy proved disastrous for Britain and France. Every passing year allowed Germany to exploit its latent economic and industrial superiority and to rearm, to the point where the democratic European powers were incapable of deterring or defeating Hitler when he finally struck. In 1940, Hitler's minister of propaganda, Joseph Goebbels, looked back on

[11] Quoted in Henry Kissinger, *Diplomacy* (New York, 1994), p. 307.

[12] As one French official stationed in Berlin put it, "If Hitler is sincere in proclaiming his desire for peace, we will be able to congratulate ourselves on having reached agreement; if he has other designs or if he has to give way one day to some fanatic we will at least have postponed the outbreak of a war and that is indeed a gain." Quoted in Anthony Adamthwaite, *France and the Coming of the Second World War, 1936–1939* (London, 1977), p. 30; Kissinger, *Diplomacy*, p. 294.

the previous two decades of European diplomacy with some amazement.

> In 1933 a French premier ought to have said (and if I had been the French premier I would have said it): "The new Reich Chancellor is the man who wrote *Mein Kampf*, which says this and that. This man cannot be tolerated in our vicinity. Either he disappears or we march!" But they didn't do it. They left us alone and let us slip through the risky zone, and we were able to sail around all dangerous reefs. *And when we were done, and well armed, better than they, then they started the war!*[13]

The sophisticated arguments of appeasement might conceivably have been more valid had they been applied to a different man and a different country under different circumstances—for instance, to the German leader of the 1920s, Gustav Stresemann. They had been misapplied to Hitler and the Germany of the 1930s. But then, in truth, the appeasement strategy had been a product not of analysis but of weakness.

If World War I severely weakened Europe, the Second World War that resulted from this failure of European strategy and diplomacy all but destroyed European nations as global powers. Their postwar inability to project sufficient force overseas to maintain colonial empires in Asia, Africa, and the Middle East forced them to retreat

[13] Quoted in Paul Johnson, *Modern Times: The World from the Twenties to the Eighties* (New York, 1983), p. 341.

on a massive scale after more than five centuries of imperial dominance—perhaps the most significant retrenchment of global influence in human history. Less than a decade into the Cold War, Europeans ceded both colonial holdings and strategic responsibilities in Asia and the Middle East to the United States, sometimes willingly and sometimes under American pressure, as in the Suez crisis.

At the end of World War II, many influential Americans had hoped that Europe could be reestablished as a "third force" in the world, strong enough to hold its own against the Soviet Union and allow the United States to pull back from Europe. Franklin Roosevelt, Dean Acheson, and other American observers believed Great Britain would shoulder the burden of defending much of the world against the Soviet Union. In those early postwar days, President Harry Truman could even imagine a world where London and Moscow competed for influence, with the United States serving as "an impartial umpire."[14] But then the British government made clear that it could not continue the economic and military support to Greece and Turkey it had been providing since the end of the war. By 1947, British officials saw that the United States would soon be "plucking the torch of world leadership from our chilling hands."[15] Europe was now dependent on the United States for its own security and for global security. France and Britain did not even like the idea of an independent European bloc, a "third force," fearing it would provide the excuse for American withdrawal from Europe.

[14] John Lewis Gaddis, *The Long Peace* (New York, 1987), p. 55.
[15] Ibid.

Once again they would be left alone facing Germany, and now the Soviet Union as well. As one American official put it, "The one faint element of confidence which [the French] cling to is the fact that American troops, however strong in number, stand between them and the Red Army."[16]

From the end of World War II and for the next fifty years, therefore, Europe fell into a state of strategic dependence on the United States. The once global reach of the European powers no longer extended beyond the Continent. Europe's sole, if vital, strategic mission during the Cold War was to stand firm and defend its own territory against any Soviet offensive until the Americans arrived. And Europeans were hard pressed to do even that. European unwillingness to spend as much on their military as American administrations believed necessary was a constant source of transatlantic tension, from the establishment of NATO to the days of Kennedy, whose doctrine of "flexible response" depended on a significant increase in European conventional forces, to the Reagan years, when American congressmen clamored for Europe to do more to "share the burden" of the common defense.

But the circumstances of the Cold War created a perhaps unavoidable tension between American and European interests. Americans generally preferred an effective European military capability—under NATO control, of course—that could stop Soviet armies on European soil short of nuclear war and with the bulk of casualties suffered by Europeans, not Americans. Not surprisingly, many

[16] Quoted in ibid., p. 65

Europeans took a different view of the most desirable form of deterrence. They were content to rely on the protection offered by the U.S. nuclear umbrella, hoping that Europe's safety could be preserved by the U.S.-Soviet balance of terror and the doctrine of mutually assured destruction. In the early years of the Cold War, European economies were too weak to build up sufficient military capacity for self-defense anyway. But even when European economies recovered later in the Cold War, the Europeans were not especially interested in closing the military gap. The American nuclear guarantee deprived Europeans of the incentive to spend the kind of money that would have been necessary to restore them to military great-power status. This psychology of dependence was also an unavoidable reality of the Cold War and the nuclear age. A proud Gaullist France might try to escape it by leaving NATO and building its own small nuclear force. But the *force de frappe* was little more than symbolism; it relieved neither France nor Europe from strategic dependence on the United States.

If Europe's relative weakness appeared less of a problem in transatlantic relations during the Cold War, it was partly because of the unique geopolitical circumstances of that conflict. Although dwarfed by the two superpowers on its flanks, a weakened Europe nevertheless served as the central strategic theater of the worldwide struggle between communism and democratic capitalism, and this, along with lingering habits of world leadership, allowed Europeans to retain international influence and international respect beyond what their sheer military capabilities might have afforded. America's Cold War strategy was built around the transatlantic alliance. Maintaining the unity and cohesion of "the West" was essential. Naturally, this elevated the importance of European opinion on global matters, giving both Europeans and Americans a perhaps exaggerated estimation of European power.

The perception persisted into the 1990s. The Balkan conflicts of that decade forced the United States to continue attending to Europe as a strategic priority. The NATO alliance appeared to have found a new, post–Cold War mission in bringing peace to that part of the Continent still prone to violent ethnic conflict, which, though on a smaller scale, appeared not unlike the century's earlier great conflicts. The enlargement of the NATO alliance to include former members of the Soviet bloc—the completion of the Cold War victory and the creation of a Europe "whole and free"—was another grand project of the West that kept Europe in the forefront of American political and strategic thinking.

And then there was the early promise of the "new" Europe. By bonding together into a single political and economic unit—the historic accomplishment of Maastricht in 1992—many hoped to recapture Europe's old greatness in a new political form. "Europe" would be the next superpower, not only economically and politically but also militarily. It would handle crises on the European continent, such as the ethnic conflicts in the Balkans, and it would reemerge as a global player of the first rank. In the 1990s, Europeans could still confidently assert that the power of a unified Europe would restore, finally, the global "multipolarity" that had been destroyed by the Cold War and its aftermath. And most Americans, with mixed emotions, agreed that superpower Europe was the future. Harvard University's Samuel P. Huntington predicted that the coalescing of the European Union would be "the single most important move" in a worldwide reaction against American hegemony and would produce a "truly multipolar" twenty-first century.[17]

Had Europe fulfilled this promise during the 1990s, the world would probably be a different place today. The United States and Europe might now be negotiating the new terms of a relationship based on a rough equality of power, instead of struggling with their vast disparity. It is possible that the product of that mutual adjustment would have been beneficial to both sides, with Europe taking on some of the burdens of global security and the United States paying greater deference to European interests and aspirations as it formulated its own foreign policies.

But the "new" Europe did not fulfill this promise. In the economic and political realms, the European Union produced miracles. Despite the hopes and fears of skeptics on both sides of the Atlantic, Europe made good on the promise of unity. And the united Europe emerged as an economic power of the first rank, able to hold its own with the United States and the Asian economies and to negotiate matters of international trade and finance on equal terms. If the end of the Cold War had ushered in an era where economic power mattered more than military power, as many in both Europe and the United States had

---

[17] Samuel P. Huntington, "The Lonely Superpower," *Foreign Affairs* 78 (March/April 1999): 35–49.

expected it would, then the European Union would indeed have been poised to shape the world order with as much influence as the United States. But the end of the Cold War did not reduce the salience of military power, and Europeans discovered that economic power did not necessarily translate into strategic and geopolitical power. The United States, which remained both an economic and a military giant, far outstripped Europe in the total power it could bring to bear on the international scene.

In fact, the 1990s witnessed not the rise of a European superpower but the further decline of Europe into relative military weakness compared to the United States. The Balkan conflict at the beginning of the decade revealed European military incapacity and political disarray; the Kosovo conflict at decade's end exposed a transatlantic gap in military technology and the ability to wage modern warfare that would only widen in subsequent years. Outside of Europe, by the close of the 1990s, the disparity was even more starkly apparent as it became clear that the ability and will of European powers, individually or collectively, to project decisive force into regions of conflict beyond the Continent were negligible. Europeans could provide peacekeeping forces in the Balkans—indeed, they eventually did provide the vast bulk of those forces in Bosnia, Kosovo, and Macedonia—and even in Afghanistan and perhaps someday in Iraq. But they lacked the wherewithal to introduce and sustain a fighting force in potentially hostile territory, even in Europe. Under the best of circumstances, the European role was limited to filling out peacekeeping forces after the United States had, largely on its own, carried out the decisive phases of a military mission and stabilized the situation. As some Europeans put it, the real division of labor consisted of the United States "making the dinner" and the Europeans "doing the dishes."

A greater American propensity to use military force did not always mean a greater willingness to risk casualties. The disparity in military capability had nothing to do with the relative courage of American and European soldiers. If anything, French and British and even German governments could sometimes be less troubled by the risks to their troops than were American presidents. During the Balkan crisis in the mid-1990s and later in Kosovo, British Prime Minister Tony Blair was more willing to put forces on the ground against Serbia than was President Bill Clinton. But in some ways this disparity, too, worked against the Europeans. The American desire to avoid casualties and the American willingness to spend heavily on new military technologies provided the United States with a formidable military capability that gave it deadly accuracy from great distances with lower risk to forces. European militaries, on the other hand, were less technologically advanced and more dependent on troops fighting in closer quarters. The effect of this technological gap, which opened wide over the course of the 1990s, when the U.S. military made remarkable advances in precision-guided munitions, joint-strike operations, and communications and intelligence gathering, only made Americans even more willing to go to war than Europeans, who lacked the ability to launch devastating attacks from safer distances and therefore had to pay a bigger price for launching any attack at all.

These European military inadequacies compared to the power of the United States should have come as no surprise, since these were characteristics of European forces during the Cold War. The strategic challenge of the Cold War and of a containment doctrine that required, in George Kennan's famous words, "adroit and vigilant counter-force at a series of constantly shifting geographical and political points" had compelled the United States to build a military force capable of projecting power into several distant regions at once.[18] Europe's strategic role had been entirely different, to defend itself and withstand the onslaught of Soviet forces, not to project power.[19] For most European powers, this required maintaining large land forces ready to block Soviet invasion routes in their own territory, not mobile forces capable of being shipped to distant regions. Americans and Europeans who proposed after the Cold War that Europe should expand its strategic role beyond the Continent were asking for a revolutionary shift in European strategy and capability. It was unrealistic to expect Europeans to return to the international great-power status they had enjoyed prior to World War II, unless European peoples were willing to shift significant resources from social to military programs and to restructure and modernize their militaries to replace

[18] X [George F. Kennan], "The Sources of Soviet Conduct," *Foreign Affairs,* July 1947, reprinted in James F. Hoge Jr. and Fareed Zakaria, eds., *The American Encounter: The United States and the Making of the Modern World* (New York, 1997), p. 165.

[19] The United Kingdom and France had the greatest capability to project force overseas, but their capacity was much smaller than that of the United States.

forces designed for passive territorial defense with forces capable of being delivered and sustained far from home.

Clearly, European voters were not willing to make such a revolutionary shift in priorities. Not only were they unwilling to pay to project force beyond Europe, but, after the Cold War, they would not pay for sufficient force to conduct even minor military actions on their own continent without American help. Nor did it seem to matter whether European publics were being asked to spend money to strengthen NATO or an independent European foreign and defense policy. Their answer was the same. Rather than viewing the collapse of the Soviet Union as an opportunity to expand Europe's strategic purview, Europeans took it as an opportunity to cash in on a sizable peace dividend. For Europe, the fall of the Soviet Union did not just eliminate a strategic adversary; in a sense, it eliminated the need for geopolitics. Many Europeans took the end of the Cold War as a holiday from strategy. Despite talk of establishing Europe as a global superpower, therefore, average European defense budgets gradually fell below 2 percent of GDP, and throughout the 1990s, European military capabilities steadily fell behind those of the United States.

The end of the Cold War had a different effect on the other side of the Atlantic. For although Americans looked for a peace dividend, too, and defense budgets declined or remained flat during most of the 1990s, defense spending still remained above 3 percent of GDP. Fast on the heels of the Soviet empire's demise came Iraq's invasion of Kuwait and the largest American military action in a quarter century—the United States deployed more than a half million soldiers to the Persian Gulf region. Thereafter

American administrations cut the Cold War force, but not as dramatically as might have been expected. In fact, successive American administrations did not view the end of the Cold War as providing a strategic holiday. From the first Bush administration through the Clinton years, American strategy and force planning continued to be based on the premise that the United States might have to fight and win two wars in different regions of the world almost simultaneously. This two-war standard, though often questioned, was never abandoned by military and civilian leaders who believed the United States did have to be prepared to fight wars on the Korean Peninsula and in the Persian Gulf. The fact that the United States could even consider maintaining such a capability set it far apart from its European allies, who on their own lacked the capacity to fight even one small war close to home, let alone two large wars thousands of miles away. By historical standards, America's post–Cold War military power, particularly its ability to project that power to all corners of the globe, remained unprecedented.

Meanwhile, the very fact of the Soviet empire's collapse vastly increased America's strength relative to the rest of the world. The sizable American military arsenal, once barely sufficient to balance Soviet power, was now deployed in a world without a single formidable adversary. This "unipolar moment" had an entirely natural and predictable consequence: It made the United States more willing to use force abroad. With the check of Soviet power removed, the United States was free to intervene practically wherever and whenever it chose—a fact reflected in the proliferation of overseas military interventions that began during the first Bush administration with the invasion of Panama in 1989, the Persian Gulf War in 1991, and the humanitarian intervention in Somalia in 1992, and continued during the Clinton years with interventions in Haiti, Bosnia, and Kosovo. While many American politicians talked of pulling back from the world, the reality was an America intervening abroad more frequently than it had throughout most of the Cold War. Thanks to the new technologies, the United States was also freer to use force around the world in more limited ways through air and missile strikes, which it did with increasing frequency. The end of the Cold War thus expanded an already wide gulf between European and American power.

PSYCHOLOGIES OF POWER
AND WEAKNESS

How could this great and growing disparity of power fail to create a growing gap in strategic perceptions and strategic "culture"? Strong powers naturally view the world differently than weaker powers. They measure risks and threats differently, they define security differently, and they have different levels of tolerance for insecurity. Those with great military power are more likely to consider force a useful tool of international relations than those who have less military power. The stronger may, in fact, rely on force more than they should. One British critic of America's propensity to military action recalls the old saw "When you have a hammer, all problems start to look like nails." This is true. But nations without great military power face the opposite danger: When you don't have a hammer, you don't want anything to look like a nail. The perspectives and psychologies of power and weakness explain much, though certainly not all, of what divides the United States and Europe today.

The problem is not new. During the Cold War, American military predominance and Europe's relative weakness produced important and sometimes serious disagreements over the U.S.-Soviet arms race and American interventions in the third world. Gaullism, *Ostpolitik*, and the various movements for European independence and unity were manifestations not only of a European desire for honor and freedom of action. They also reflected a European conviction that America's approach to the Cold War was too confrontational, too militaristic, and too dangerous. After the very early years of the Cold War, when Churchill and others sometimes worried that the United States was too gentle in dealing with Stalin, it was usually the Americans who pushed for tougher forms of containment and the Europeans who resisted. The Europeans believed they knew better how to deal with the Soviets: through engagement and seduction, through commercial and political ties, through patience and forbearance. It was a legitimate view, shared at times by many Americans, especially during and after the Vietnam War, when American leaders believed they, too, were working from a position of weakness. But Europeans' repeated dissent from the harder American approach to the Cold War reflected Europe's fundamental and enduring weakness relative to the United States: Europe simply had fewer military options at its disposal, and it was more vulnerable to a powerful

Soviet Union. The European approach may have reflected, too, Europe's memory of continental war. Americans, when they were not themselves engaged in the subtleties of détente, viewed the European approach as a new form of appeasement, a return to the fearful mentality of the 1930s. Europeans viewed it as a policy of sophistication, as a possible escape from what they regarded as Washington's excessively confrontational approach to the Cold War.

During the Cold War, however, these were more tactical than philosophical disagreements. They were not arguments about the purposes of power, since both sides of the Atlantic clearly relied on their pooled military power to deter any possible Soviet attack, no matter how remote the chances of such an attack might seem. The end of the Cold War, which both widened the power gap and removed the common Soviet enemy, not only exacerbated the difference in strategic perspectives but also changed the nature of the argument.

For much of the 1990s, nostalgic policymakers and analysts on both sides of the Atlantic insisted that Americans and Europeans mostly agreed on the nature of these threats to peace and world order; where they disagreed was on the question of how to respond. This sunny analysis overlooked the growing divide. More and more over the past decade, the United States and its European allies have had rather substantial disagreements over what constitute intolerable threats to international security and the world order, as the case of Iraq has abundantly shown. And these disagreements reflect, above all, the disparity of power.

One of the biggest transatlantic disagreements since the end of the Cold War has been over which "new" threats merit the most attention. American administrations have placed the greatest emphasis on so-called rogue states and what President George W. Bush a year ago called the "axis of evil." Most Europeans have taken a calmer view of the risks posed by these regimes. As a French official once told me, "The problem is 'failed states,' not 'rogue states.' "

Why should Americans and Europeans view the same threats differently? Europeans often argue that Americans have an unreasonable demand for "perfect" security, the product of living for centuries shielded behind two oceans.[20] Europeans claim they know what it is like to live with danger, to exist side by side with evil, since they've done it for centuries—hence their greater tolerance for such threats as may be posed by Saddam Hussein's Iraq, the ayatollahs' Iran, or North Korea. Americans, they claim, make far too much of the dangers these regimes pose.

But there is less to this cultural explanation than meets the eye. The United States in its formative decades lived in a state of substantial insecurity, surrounded by hostile European empires on the North American continent, at constant risk of being torn apart by centrifugal forces that were encouraged by threats from without: National insecurity formed the core of George Washington's Farewell Address. As for the Europeans' supposed tolerance for insecurity and evil, it can be overstated. For the better part of three centuries, European Catholics and Protestants

[20] For that matter, this is also the view commonly found in American textbooks.

more often preferred to kill than to tolerate each other; nor have the past two centuries shown all that much mutual tolerance between French and Germans. Some Europeans argue that precisely because Europe has suffered so much, it has a higher tolerance for suffering than America and therefore a higher tolerance for threats. More likely the opposite is true. The memory of the First World War made the British and French publics more fearful of Nazi Germany, not more tolerant, and this attitude contributed significantly to the appeasement strategy of the 1930s.

A better explanation of Europe's greater tolerance for threats today is its relative weakness. The differing psychologies of power and weakness are easy enough to understand. A man armed only with a knife may decide that a bear prowling the forest is a tolerable danger, inasmuch as the alternative—hunting the bear armed only with a knife—is actually riskier than lying low and hoping the bear never attacks. The same man armed with a rifle, however, will likely make a different calculation of what constitutes a tolerable risk. Why should he risk being mauled to death if he doesn't have to? This perfectly normal human psychology has driven a wedge between the United States and Europe. The vast majority of Europeans always believed that the threat posed by Saddam Hussein was more tolerable than the risk of removing him. But Americans, being stronger, developed a lower threshold of tolerance for Saddam and his weapons of mass destruction, especially after September 11. Both assessments made sense, given the differing perspectives of a powerful America and a weaker Europe. Europeans like

to say that Americans are obsessed with fixing problems, but it is generally true that those with a greater
capacity to fix problems are more likely to try to fix them
than those who have no such capability. Americans could
imagine successfully invading Iraq and toppling Saddam, and therefore by the end of 2002 more than 70 percent of Americans favored such action. Not surprisingly,
Europeans found the prospect both unimaginable and
frightening.

The incapacity to respond to threats leads not only to
tolerance. It can also lead to denial. It is normal to try to
put out of one's mind that which one can do nothing
about. According to one student of European opinion,
even the very focus on "threats" differentiates American
policymakers from their European counterparts. Americans, writes Steven Everts, talk about foreign "threats"
such as "the proliferation of weapons of mass destruction,
terrorism, and 'rogue states.' " But Europeans look at
"challenges," such as "ethnic conflict, migration, organized
crime, poverty and environmental degradation." As Everts
notes, however, the key difference is less a matter of culture and philosophy than of capability. Europeans "are
most worried about issues . . . that have a greater chance of
being solved by political engagement and huge sums of
money."[21] In other words, Europeans focus on issues—
"challenges"—where European strengths come into play,
but not on those "threats" where European weakness

[21] Steven Everts, "Unilateral America, Lightweight Europe?: Managing Divergence in Transatlantic Foreign Policy," working paper,
Centre for European Reform, February 2001.

ROBERT KAGAN

makes solutions elusive. If Europe's strategic culture today places less value on hard power and military strength and more value on such soft-power tools as economics and trade, isn't it partly because Europe is militarily weak and economically strong? Americans are quicker to acknowledge the existence of threats, even to perceive them where others may not see any, because they can conceive of doing something to meet those threats.

The differing threat perceptions in the United States and Europe are not just matters of psychology, however. They are also grounded in a practical reality that is another product of the disparity of power and the structure of the present international order. For while Iraq and other rogue states have posed a threat to Europe, objectively they have *not* posed the same level of threat to Europeans as they have to the United States. There is, first of all, the American security guarantee that Europeans enjoy and have enjoyed for six decades, ever since the United States took upon itself the burden of maintaining order in far-flung regions of the world—from East Asia to the Middle East—from which European power had largely withdrawn. Europeans have generally believed, whether or not they admit it to themselves, that whenever Iraq or some other rogue nation emerged as a real and present danger, as opposed to merely a potential danger, then the United States would do something about it. If during the Cold War Europe by necessity made a major contribution to its own defense, since the end of the Cold War Europeans have enjoyed an unparalleled measure of "free security" because most of the likely threats emanate from regions outside Europe, where only the United States can project effective force. In a very practical sense—that is, when it comes to actual strategic planning—Iraq, North Korea, Iran, or any other rogue state in the world has not been primarily a European problem. Nor, certainly, is China. Both Europeans and Americans agree that these are primarily American problems.

This is why Saddam Hussein was never perceived to be the threat to Europe that he was to the United States. The logical consequence of the transatlantic disparity of power has been that the task of containing Saddam Hussein always belonged primarily to the United States, not to Europe, and everyone agreed on this[22]—including Saddam, which was why he always considered the United States, not Europe, his principal adversary. In the Persian Gulf, the Middle East, and most other regions of the world (including Europe), the United States plays the role of ultimate enforcer. "You are so powerful," Europeans often say to Americans. "So why do you feel so threatened?" But it is precisely America's great power and its willingness to assume the responsibility for protecting other nations that make it the primary target, and often the only target. Most Europeans have been understandably content that it should remain so.

A poll of European and American opinion taken in the summer of 2002 nicely revealed this transatlantic gap in perceptions of threat. Although widely reported as showing American and European publics in rough agreement, the results indicated many more Americans than Euro-

---

[22] Notwithstanding the sizable British contribution to military operations in Iraq.

peans worried about the threat posed not only by Iraq, Iran, and North Korea, but also by China, Russia, the India-Pakistan confrontation, and even the conflict between Israel and the Arab states—on almost all these issues significantly more Americans than Europeans expressed concern.[23] But why should Americans, "protected by two oceans," be more worried about a conflagration on the Asian subcontinent or in the Middle East or in Russia than the Europeans, who live so much closer? The answer is that Americans know that when international crises erupt, whether in the Taiwan Strait or in Kashmir, they are likely to be the first to become involved. Europeans know this, too. Polls that show Americans worrying more than Europeans about all nature of global security threats and Europeans worrying more about global warming demonstrate that both sets of publics have a remarkably accurate sense of their nations' very different global roles.

Americans are "cowboys," Europeans love to say. And there is truth in this. The United States does act as an international sheriff, self-appointed perhaps but widely

[23] The poll, sponsored by the German Marshall Fund and the Chicago Council on Foreign Relations, was taken between June 1 and July 6, 2002. Asked to identify which "possible threats to vital interests" were "extremely important," 91 percent of Americans listed "international terrorism" as opposed to 65 percent of Europeans. On "Iraq developing weapons of mass destruction," the gap was 28 points, with 86 percent of Americans identifying Iraq as an "extremely important" threat compared to 58 percent of Europeans. On "Islamic fundamentalism," 61–49; on "military conflict between Israel and Arab neighbors," 67–43; on "tensions between India and Pakistan," 54–32; on "development of China as a world power," 56–19; on "political turmoil in Russia," 27–15.

welcomed nevertheless, trying to enforce some peace and justice in what Americans see as a lawless world where outlaws need to be deterred or destroyed, often through the muzzle of a gun. Europe, by this Wild West analogy, is more like the saloonkeeper. Outlaws shoot sheriffs, not saloonkeepers. In fact, from the saloonkeeper's point of view, the sheriff trying to impose order by force can sometimes be more threatening than the outlaws, who, at least for the time being, may just want a drink.

When Europeans took to the streets by the millions after September 11, most Americans believed it was out of a sense of shared danger and common interest: The Europeans knew they could be next. But Europeans by and large did not feel that way. Europeans have never really believed they are next. They could be secondary targets—because they are allied with the United States— but they are not the primary target, because they no longer play the imperial role in the Middle East that might have engendered the same antagonism against them as is aimed at the United States. When Europeans wept and waved American flags after September 11, it was out of genuine human sympathy. It was an expression of sorrow and affection for Americans. For better or for worse, European displays of solidarity were a product more of fellow feeling than of careful calculations of self-interest. Europeans' heartfelt sympathy, unaccompanied by a sense of shared risk and common responsibility, did not draw Europeans and Americans together in strategic partnership. On the contrary, as soon as Americans began looking beyond the immediate task of finding and destroying

Osama bin Laden and Al Qaeda to broader strategic goals in the "war on terrorism," Europeans recoiled.

Differing perceptions of threats and how to address them are in some ways only the surface manifestation of more fundamental differences in the worldviews of a strong United States and a relatively weaker Europe. It is not just that Europeans and Americans have not shared the same view of what to do about a specific problem such as Iraq. They do not share the same broad view of how the world should be governed, about the role of international institutions and international law, about the proper balance between the use of force and the use of diplomacy in international affairs.

Some of this difference is related to the power gap. Europe's relative weakness has understandably produced a powerful European interest in building a world where military strength and hard power matter less than economic and soft power, an international order where international law and international institutions matter more than the power of individual nations, where unilateral action by powerful states is forbidden, where all nations regardless of their strength have equal rights and are equally protected by commonly agreed-upon international rules of behavior. Because they are relatively weak, Europeans have a deep interest in devaluing and eventually eradicating the brutal laws of an anarchic Hobbesian world where power is the ultimate determinant of national security and success.

This is no reproach. It is what weaker powers have wanted from time immemorial. It was what Americans wanted in the eighteenth and early nineteenth centuries, when the brutality of a European system of power politics run by the global giants of France, Britain, and Russia left Americans constantly vulnerable to imperial thrashing. It was what the other small powers of Europe wanted in those years, too, only to be sneered at by Bourbon kings and other powerful monarchs, who spoke instead of *raison d'état*. The great proponent of international law on the high seas in the eighteenth century was the United States; the great opponent was Britain's navy, the "mistress of the seas." In an anarchic world, small powers always fear they will be victims. Great powers, on the other hand, often fear rules that may constrain them more than they do anarchy. In an anarchic world, they rely on their power to provide security and prosperity.

This natural and historic disagreement between the stronger and the weaker manifests itself in today's transatlantic dispute over the issue of unilateralism. Europeans generally believe their objection to American unilateralism is proof of their greater commitment to principles of world order. And it is true that their commitment to those ideals, although not absolute, is greater than that of most Americans. But Europeans are less willing to acknowledge another truth: that their hostility to unilateralism is also self-interested. Since Europeans lack the capacity to undertake unilateral military actions, either individually or collectively as "Europe," it is natural that they should oppose allowing others to do what they cannot do themselves. For Europeans, the appeal to multilateralism and international law has a real practical payoff and little cost.

The same cannot be said of the United States. Polls

consistently show that Americans support multilateral action in principle. They even support acting under the rubric of the United Nations, which, after all, Americans created. But the fact remains that the United States can act unilaterally and has done so many times with reasonable success. The facile assertion that the United States cannot "go it alone" is more a hopeful platitude than a description of reality. Americans certainly prefer to act together with others, and American actions stand a better chance of success if the United States has allies. But if it were literally true that the United States could not act unilaterally, we wouldn't be having a grand transatlantic debate over American unilateralism. The problem today, if it is a problem, is that the United States *can* "go it alone," and it is hardly surprising that the American superpower should wish to preserve its ability to do so. Geopolitical logic dictates that Americans have a less compelling interest than Europeans in upholding multilateralism as a universal principle for governing the behavior of nations. Whether unilateral action is a good or a bad thing, Americans objectively have more to lose from outlawing it than any other power in today's unipolar world. Indeed, for Americans to share the European perspective on the virtues of multilateralism, they would have to be even more devoted to the ideals and principles of an international legal order than Europeans are. For Europeans, ideals and interests converge in a world governed according to the principle of multilateralism. For Americans, they do not converge as much.

It is also understandable that Europeans should fear American unilateralism and seek to constrain it as best they can through such institutions as the United Nations. Those who cannot act unilaterally themselves naturally want to have a mechanism for controlling those who can. From the European perspective, the United States may be a relatively benign hegemon, but insofar as its actions delay the arrival of a world order more conducive to the safety of weaker powers, it is objectively dangerous. This is one reason why in recent years a principal objective of European foreign policy has become, as one European observer puts it, the "multilateralising" of the United States.[24] It is why Europeans insist that the United States act only with the approval of the UN Security Council. The Security Council is a pale approximation of a genuine multilateral order, for it was designed by the United States to give the five "great powers" of the postwar era an exclusive authority to decide what was and was not legitimate international action. Today the Security Council contains only one "great power," the United States. But the Security Council is nevertheless the one place where a weaker nation such as France has at least the theoretical power to control American actions, *if* the United States can be persuaded to come to the Security Council and be bound by its decisions. For Europeans, the UN Security Council is a substitute for the power they lack.

Indeed, despite the predictions of Huntington and many realist theorists, the Europeans have not sought to check the rising power of the American colossus by amassing a countervailing power of their own. Clearly

[24] Everts, "Unilateral America, Lightweight Europe?"

they do not consider even a unilateralist United States a sufficient threat to make them increase defense spending to contain it. Nor are they willing to risk their vast trade with the United States by attempting to wield their economic power against the hegemon. Nor are they willing to ally themselves with China, which is willing to spend money on defense, in order to counterbalance the United States. Instead, Europeans hope to contain American power without wielding power themselves. In what may be the ultimate feat of subtlety and indirection, they want to control the behemoth by appealing to its conscience.

It is a sound strategy, as far as it goes. The United States *is* a behemoth with a conscience. It is not Louis XIV's France or George III's England. Americans do not argue, even to themselves, that their actions may be justified by *raison d'état*. They do not claim the right of the stronger or insist to the rest of the world, as the Athenians did at Melos, that "the strong rule where they can and the weak suffer what they must." Americans have never accepted the principles of Europe's old order nor embraced the Machiavellian perspective. The United States is a liberal, progressive society through and through, and to the extent that Americans believe in power, they believe it must be a means of advancing the principles of a liberal civilization and a liberal world order. Americans even share Europe's aspirations for a more orderly world system based not on power but on rules—after all, they were striving for such a world when Europeans were still extolling the laws of *Machtpolitik*. But while these common ideals and aspirations shape foreign policies on both sides of the Atlantic, they cannot completely negate the very different perspectives from which Europeans and Americans view the world and the role of power in international affairs.

HYPERPUISSANCE

The present transatlantic tensions did not begin with the inauguration of George W. Bush in January 2001, nor did they begin after September 11. While the ham-handed diplomacy of the Bush administration in its early months certainly drew a sharper line under the differing European and American perspectives on the issues of international governance, and while the attacks of September 11 shone the brightest possible light on the transatlantic gulf in strategic perceptions, those divisions were already evident during the Clinton years and even during the first Bush administration. As early as 1992, mutual recriminations had been rife over Bosnia. The first Bush administration refused to act, believing it had more important strategic obligations elsewhere. Europeans declared they would act—it was, they insisted, "the hour of Europe"—but the declaration proved hollow when it became clear that Europe could not act even in Bosnia without the United States. When France and Germany took the first small steps to create something like an independent European defense force, the Bush administration scowled. From the European point of view, it was the worst of both worlds. The United States was losing interest in preserving European security, but at the same time it was hostile to European aspirations to take on the task themselves.[25] Europeans complained about American perfidy, and Americans complained about European weakness and ingratitude.

Today many Europeans view the Clinton years as a time of transatlantic harmony, but it was during those years that Europeans began complaining about American power and arrogance in the post–Cold War world. It was during the Clinton years that then–French foreign minister Hubert Védrine coined the term *hyperpuissance* to describe an American behemoth too worryingly powerful to be designated merely a superpower. And it was during the 1990s that Europeans began to view the United States as a "hectoring hegemon." Such complaints were directed especially at Secretary of State Madeleine Albright, whom one American critic described, a bit hyperbolically, as "the first Secretary of State in American history whose diplomatic specialty . . . is lecturing other governments, using threatening language and tastelessly bragging of the power and virtue of her country."[26]

Even in the 1990s the issue on which American and European policies began most notably to diverge was Iraq. Europeans were appalled when Albright and other administration officials in 1997 began suggesting that the eco-

[25] Charles Grant, "European Defence Post-Kosovo?," working paper, Centre for European Reform, June 1999, p. 2.

[26] The comment was by former State Department adviser Charles Maechling Jr., quoted in Thomas W. Lippman, *Madeleine Albright and the New American Diplomacy* (Boulder, CO, 2000), p. 165.

nomic sanctions placed on Iraq after the Gulf War could not be lifted while Saddam Hussein remained in power. They believed, in classically European fashion, that Iraq should be offered incentives for better behavior, not threatened, in classically American fashion, with more economic or military coercion. The growing split between the United States and its allies on the Iraq question came into the open at the end of 1997, when the Clinton administration tried to increase the pressure on Baghdad to cooperate with UN arms inspectors, and France joined Russia and China in blocking the American proposals in the UN Security Council. When the Clinton administration finally turned to the use of military force and bombed Iraq in December 1998, it did so without a UN Security Council authorization and with only Great Britain by its side. In its waning months, the Clinton administration continued to believe that "Iraq, under Saddam Hussein, remains dangerous, unreconstructed, defiant, and isolated." It would "never be able to be rehabilitated or reintegrated into the community of nations" with Saddam in power.[27] This was not the view of France or most of the rest of Europe. The rehabilitation and reintegration of Saddam Hussein's Iraq were precisely what they sought.

It was during the 1990s, too, that some of the contentious issues that would produce transatlantic storms during the second Bush administration made their first appearance. Clinton took the first steps toward construct-

[27] Address by Assistant Secretary of State Martin Indyk to the Council on Foreign Relations, April 22, 1999, quoted in ibid., p. 183.

ROBERT KAGAN

ing a new missile defense system designed to protect the United States from nuclear-armed rogue states such as North Korea. Such a system threatened to undo the Antiballistic Missile Treaty and the doctrine of mutually assured destruction that Europeans had long valued as central to their own strategic security. It also threatened to protect American soil while leaving Europeans still vulnerable to nuclear attack, which Europeans understandably considered undesirable. The Clinton administration negotiated the Kyoto protocol to address global climate change but deliberately did not submit it to the Senate, where it was certain to be defeated. And it was the Clinton administration, prodded by Secretary of Defense William Cohen and senior military officials at the Pentagon, that first demanded that American troops be immune from prosecution by the new International Criminal Court—which had become the quintessential symbol of European aspirations to a world in which all nations were equal under the law. In taking this tack away from the European multilateralist consensus, President Clinton was to some extent bowing to pressures from a hostile Republican-dominated Congress. But the Clinton administration itself believed those treaties were flawed; even Clinton was not as "European" as he would later be depicted. In any case, the growing divergence between American and European policies during the Clinton years reflected a deeper reality. The United States in the post–Cold War era was becoming more unilateral in its approach to the rest of the world at a time when Europeans were embarking on a new and vigorous effort to build a more comprehensive international legal system precisely to restrain such unilateralism.

The war in Kosovo in the spring of 1999 gave an interesting hint of the future. Although the allied military campaign against Serbia's Slobodan Milosevic was a success, and represented the first occasion in its fifty-year history that NATO had ever undertaken military action, the conflict also revealed subtle fissures in the post–Cold War alliance—fissures that survived Kosovo but might not withstand the greater pressures of a different kind of war under different international circumstances.

The conduct of the war reflected the severe transatlantic military imbalance. The United States flew the majority of missions, almost all of the precision-guided munitions dropped in Serbia and Kosovo were made in America, and the unmatched superiority of American technical intelligence-gathering capabilities meant that 99 percent of the proposed targets came from American intelligence sources. The American dominance of the war effort troubled Europeans in two ways. On the one hand, it was a rather shocking blow to European honor. As two British analysts observed after the war, even the United Kingdom, "which prides itself on being a serious military power, could contribute only 4 per cent of the aircraft and 4 per cent of the bombs dropped."[28] To Europe's most respected strategic thinkers in France, Germany, and Britain, the Kosovo war had only "highlighted the impotence of Europe's armed forces." It was embarrassing

[28] Tim Garden and John Roper, "Pooling Forces," Centre for European Reform, December 1999.

that even in a region as close as the Balkans, Europe's "ability to deploy force" was but "a meager fraction" of America's.[29]

More troubling still was that European dependence on American military power gave the United States dominant influence not only over the way the war was fought but also over international diplomacy before, during, and after the war. Europeans had favored a pause in the bombing after a few days, for instance, to give Milosevic a chance to end the crisis. But the United States and the American NATO commander, General Wesley K. Clark, refused. Most Europeans, especially the French, wanted to escalate the bombing campaign gradually, to reduce the damage to Serbia and give Milosevic incentive to end the conflict before NATO destroyed everything he valued. But Clark disagreed. "In U.S. military thinking," he explains, "we seek to be as decisive as possible once we begin to use force."[30] Many Europeans wanted to focus the bombing on Serbian forces engaged in "ethnic cleansing" in Kosovo. But as Clark recalls, "Most Americans believed that the best and most rapid way to change Milosevic's views was to strike at him and his regime as hard as possible."[31]

Whether the Americans or the Europeans were right about the way that war or any war should be fought, for Europe the depressing fact remained that because the

[29] Christoph Bertram, Charles Grant, and François Heisbourg, "European Defence: The Next Steps," Centre for European Reform, *CER Bulletin* 14 (October/November 2000).

[30] Wesley K. Clark, *Waging Modern War* (New York, 2001), p. 449.

[31] Americans also didn't want their pilots flying at low altitudes where they were more likely to be shot down. Ibid.

Kosovo war was fought with "American equipment," it was fought largely according to "American doctrine."[32] For all Europe's great economic power and for all its success at achieving political union, Europe's military weakness had produced diplomatic weakness and sharply diminished its political influence compared to that of the United States, even in a crisis in Europe.

The Americans were unhappy, too. General Clark and his colleagues complained that the laborious effort to preserve consensus within the alliance hampered the fighting of the war and delayed its successful conclusion. Before the war, Clark later insisted, "we could not present an unambiguous and clear warning to Milosevic," partly because many European countries would not threaten action without a mandate from the UN Security Council—what Clark, in typically American fashion, called Europe's "legal issues." For the Americans, these "legal issues" were "obstacles to properly planning and preparing" for the war.[33] During the fighting, Clark and his American colleagues were exasperated by the need constantly to find compromise between American military doctrine and what Clark called the "European approach."[34] "It was always the Americans who pushed for the escalation to new, more sensitive targets . . . and always some of the Allies who expressed doubts and reservations." In

[32] Garden and Roper, "Pooling Forces."

[33] Clark, *Waging Modern War*, pp. 420, 421. "The lack of legal authority," Clark recalls, "caused almost every NATO government initially to reject Secretary Cohen's appeal to authorize a NATO threat" prior to the outbreak of war in early 1999.

[34] Ibid., p. 449.

Clark's view, "We paid a price in operational effectiveness by having to constrain the nature of the operation to fit within the political and legal concerns of NATO member nations."[35] The result was a war that neither Europeans nor Americans liked. In a meeting of NATO defense ministers a few months after the war, one minister remarked that the biggest lesson of the allied war in Kosovo was that "we never want to do this again."[36]

Fortunately for the health of the alliance in 1999, Clark and his superiors in the Clinton administration believed the price for allied unity was worth paying. But American willingness to preserve transatlantic cohesion even at the cost of military effectiveness owed a great deal to the special, if not unique, circumstances of the Kosovo conflict. For the United States, preserving the cohesion and viability of the alliance was not just a means to an end in Kosovo; it was among the primary aims of the American intervention, just as saving the alliance had been a primary motive for America's earlier intervention in Bosnia, and just as preserving the cohesion of the alliance had been a primary goal of American strategy during the Cold War.

American abstention from the Balkan conflict during the first Bush administration and in Clinton's first term had seemed to threaten NATO itself. When Secretary of State James Baker referred to the Balkan war as a strictly "European conflict" and declared that the United States did not have "a dog in that fight," such sentiments, widely

35 Ibid., p. 426.
36 As Clark wryly reports, "No one laughed." Ibid., p. 417.

shared among his colleagues, including especially then–
Chairman of the Joint Chiefs of Staff Colin Powell, had
raised troubling questions about America's role in Europe
in the post–Cold War world. Was the United States still
committed to European security and stability? Could
NATO meet what were then considered to be the new
challenges of the post–Cold War era, ethnic conflict and
the collapse of states? Or had the American-led alliance
outlived its usefulness to the point where it could not stop
aggression and ethnic cleansing even on the European
continent?

American involvement in Kosovo or Bosnia was not
based on calculations of a narrow American "national
interest," at least as most Americans understood the term.
While Americans had a compelling moral interest in stop-
ping genocide and ethnic cleansing, especially in Europe,
American realist theorists insisted the United States had
no "national interest" at stake in the Balkans. When Clinton officials and other supporters of American intervention defended American military action on the grounds of
the national interest, it was as a means of preserving the
alliance and repairing the frayed bonds of the transatlantic relationship. As in the Cold War, America fought
in the Balkans ultimately to preserve "the West." And that
goal determined American military strategy. As General
Clark puts it, "No single target or set of targets was more
important than NATO cohesion."[37]

Such an approach to fighting the war may have been
sound in Kosovo and Bosnia. But it raised questions about

[37] Ibid., p. 430.

the future. Would Clark or any future American commander make the same calculation in different circumstances? Would he be willing to sacrifice operational effectiveness, rapid escalation, "American military doctrine," and the use of decisive force in a war whose primary goal was not the cohesion and preservation of NATO and Europe? In fact, the Kosovo war showed how difficult it was going to be for the United States and its European allies to fight any war together. What if they had to fight a war not primarily "humanitarian" in nature? What if Americans believed their vital interests were directly threatened? What if Americans had suffered horrendous attacks on their own territory and feared more attacks were coming? Would Americans in such circumstances have the same tolerance for the clumsy and constrained NATO decision-making and war-fighting process? Would they want to compromise again with the "European approach" to warfare, or would they prefer to "go it alone"? The answer to those questions came after September 11. With almost three thousand dead in New York City, and Osama bin Laden on the loose in Afghanistan, the U.S. military and the Bush administration had little interest in working through NATO. This may have been unfortunate from the perspective of transatlantic relations, but it was hardly surprising.

The fact is that by the end of the 1990s the disparity of power was subtly rending the fabric of the transatlantic relationship. The Americans were unhappy and impatient about constraints imposed by European allies who brought so little to a war but whose concern for "legal issues" prevented the war's effective prosecution. The

Europeans were unhappy about American dominance and their own dependence. The lesson for Americans, including the top officials in the Clinton administration, was that even with the best intentions, multilateral action could not succeed without a significant element of American unilateralism, an American willingness to use its overwhelming power to dominate both war and diplomacy when weaker allies hesitated. The Clinton administration had come into office talking about "assertive multilateralism"; it ended up talking about America as "the indispensable nation."

The lesson for many Europeans was that Europe needed to take steps to release itself at least partially from a dependence on American power that, after the Cold War, seemed no longer necessary. This, in turn, required that Europe create some independent military capability. At the end of 1998, that judgment prompted no less a friend of the United States than Tony Blair to reach across the Channel to France with an unprecedented offer to add Britain's weight to hitherto stalled efforts to create a common European Union defense capability independent of NATO. Together, Blair and Jacques Chirac won Europe-wide approval for building a force of 60,000 troops that could be deployed far from home and sustained for up to a year.

Once again, had this Anglo-French initiative borne fruit, the United States and Europe might today be in the process of establishing a new relationship based on a greater European military capability and greater independence from American power. But this initiative is headed the way of all other proposals to enhance European military power and strategic self-reliance. In December 2001 the Belgian foreign minister suggested that the EU military force should simply "declare itself operational without such a declaration being based on any true capability."[38] In fact, the effort to build a European force has so far been an embarrassment to Europeans. Today, the European Union is no closer to fielding an independent force, even a small one, than it was three years ago. And this latest failure raises the question that so many Europeans and so many "transatlanticists" in the United States have been unwilling even to ask, much less to answer: Why hasn't Europe fulfilled the promise of the European Union in foreign and defense policy, or met the promptings of some of its most important leaders to build up even enough military power to tilt the balance, just a little, away from American dominance?

THE POSTMODERN PARADISE

The answer lies somewhere in the realm of ideology, in European attitudes not just toward defense spending but toward power itself. Important as the power gap has been in shaping the respective strategic cultures of the United States and Europe, if the disparity of military capabilities were the only problem, the solution would be fairly straightforward. With a highly educated and productive population of almost 400 million people and a $9 trillion economy, Europe today has the wealth and technological

[38] John Vinocur, "On Both War and Peace, the EU Stands Divided," *International Herald Tribune,* December 17, 2001.

capability to make itself more of a world power in military terms if Europeans wanted to become that kind of world power. They could easily spend twice as much as they are currently spending on defense if they believed it necessary to do so.[39] And closing the power gap between the United States and Europe would probably go some way toward closing the gap in strategic perceptions.

There is a cynical view current in American strategic circles that the Europeans simply enjoy the "free ride" they have gotten under the American security umbrella over the past six decades. Given America's willingness to spend so much money protecting them, Europeans would rather spend their own money on social welfare programs, long vacations, and shorter workweeks. But there is more to the transatlantic gulf than a gap in military capabilities, and while Europe may be enjoying a free ride in terms of global security, there is more to Europe's unwillingness to build up its military power than comfort with the present American guarantee. After all, the United States in the nineteenth century was the beneficiary of the British navy's dominance of the Atlantic and the Caribbean. But that did not stop the United States from engaging in its own peacetime naval buildup in the 1880s and 1890s, a buildup that equipped it to launch and win the Spanish-

---

[39] Europeans insist that there are certain structural realities in their national budgets, built-in limitations to any significant increases in defense spending. But if Europe were about to be invaded, would its politicians insist that defense budgets could not be raised because this would violate the terms of the EU's growth and stability pact? If Germans truly felt threatened, would they insist nevertheless that their social welfare programs be left untouched?

American War, acquire the Philippines, and become a world power. Late-nineteenth-century Americans did not take comfort from their security; they were ambitious for more power.

Europeans today are not ambitious for power, and certainly not for military power. Europeans over the past half century have developed a genuinely different perspective on the role of power in international relations, a perspective that springs directly from their unique historical experience since the end of World War II. They have rejected the power politics that brought them such misery over the past century and more. This is a perspective on power that Americans do not and cannot share, inasmuch as the formative historical experiences on their side of the Atlantic have not been the same.

Consider again the qualities that make up the European strategic culture: the emphasis on negotiation, diplomacy, and commercial ties, on international law over the use of force, on seduction over coercion, on multilateralism over unilateralism. It is true that these are not traditionally European approaches to international relations when viewed from a long historical perspective. But they are a product of more recent European history. The modern European strategic culture represents a conscious rejection of the European past, a rejection of the evils of European *Machtpolitik*. It is a reflection of Europeans' ardent and understandable desire never to return to that past. Who knows better than Europeans the dangers that arise from unbridled power politics, from an excessive reliance on military force, from policies produced by national egoism and ambition, even from balance of power and *raison d'état*? As German Foreign Minister Joschka Fischer put it in a speech outlining his vision of the European future, "The core of the concept of Europe after 1945 was and still is a rejection of the European balance-of-power principle and the hegemonic ambitions of individual states that had emerged following the Peace of Westphalia in 1648."[40] The European Union is itself the product of an awful century of European warfare.

Of course, it was the "hegemonic ambitions" of one nation in particular that European integration was meant to contain. And it is the integration and taming of Germany that is the great accomplishment of Europe—viewed historically, perhaps the greatest feat of international politics ever achieved. Some Europeans recall, as Fischer does, the central role the United States played in solving the "German problem." Fewer like to recall that the military destruction of Nazi Germany was the prerequisite for the European peace that followed. Instead, most Europeans like to believe that it was the transformation of the European mind and spirit that made possible the "new order." The Europeans, who invented power politics, turned themselves into born-again idealists by an act of will, leaving behind them what Fischer called "the old system of balance with its continued national orientation, constraints of coalition, traditional interest-led politics and the permanent danger of nationalist ideologies and confrontations."

Fischer stands near one end of the spectrum of European idealism. But this is not really a right-left issue in Europe. Fischer's principal contention—that Europe has

[40] Fischer speech at Humboldt University in Berlin, May 12, 2000.

moved beyond the old system of power politics and discovered a new system for preserving peace in international
relations—is widely shared across Europe. As senior British
diplomat and EU official Robert Cooper has argued,
Europe today lives in a "postmodern system" that does not
rest on a balance of power but on "the rejection of force"
and on "self-enforced rules of behavior." In the "postmodern world," writes Cooper, "*raison d'état* and the amorality
of Machiavelli's theories of statecraft . . . have been replaced
by a moral consciousness" in international affairs.[41]

American realists might scoff at this idealism. Hans
Morgenthau and George Kennan assumed that only naïve
Americans succumbed to such "Wilsonian" legalistic and
moralistic fancies, not those war-tested, historically minded
European Machiavels. But, really, why shouldn't Europeans be idealistic about international affairs, at least
as they are conducted in Europe's "postmodern system"?
Within the confines of Europe, the age-old laws of international relations have been repealed. Europeans have
pursued their new order, freed from the laws and even the
mentality of power politics. Europeans have stepped out
of the Hobbesian world of anarchy into the Kantian world
of perpetual peace.

In fact, the United States solved the Kantian paradox
for the Europeans. Kant had argued that the only solution
to the immoral horrors of the Hobbesian world was the
creation of a world government. But he also feared that
the "state of universal peace" made possible by world government would be an even greater threat to human free-

[41] Robert Cooper, *The Observer*, April 7, 2002.

dom than the Hobbesian international order, inasmuch as such a government, with its monopoly of power, would become "the most horrible despotism."[42] How nations could achieve perpetual peace without destroying human freedom was a problem Kant could not solve. But for Europe the problem was solved by the United States. By providing security from outside, the United States rendered it unnecessary for Europe's supranational government to provide it. Europeans did not need power to achieve peace, and they do not need power to preserve it.

European life during the more than five decades since the end of World War II has been shaped not by the brutal laws of power politics but by the unfolding of a geopolitical fantasy, a miracle of world-historical importance: The German lion has lain down with the French lamb. The conflict that ravaged Europe ever since the violent birth of Germany in the nineteenth century has been put to rest. The means by which this miracle has been achieved have understandably acquired something of a sacred mystique for Europeans, especially since the end of the Cold War. Diplomacy, negotiations, patience, the forging of economic ties, political engagement, the use of inducements rather than sanctions, compromise rather than confrontation, the taking of small steps and tempering ambitions for success—these were the tools of Franco-German rapprochement and hence the tools that made European integration possible. France, in particular, took the leap into the unknown, offering to pool first economic and

[42] See Thomas L. Pangle and Peter J. Ahrensdorf, *Justice Among Nations: On the Moral Basis of Power and Peace* (Lawrence, KS, 1999), pp. 200–201.

then political sovereignty with its old German enemy as the best means of preventing future conflicts. Germany, in turn, ceded its own great power within Europe in the interest of reintegration.

The integration of Europe was not to be based on military deterrence or the balance of power. To the contrary, the miracle came from the rejection of military power and of its utility as an instrument of international affairs—at least within the confines of Europe. During the Cold War, few Europeans doubted the need for military power to deter the Soviet Union. But the end of the Cold War, by removing even the external danger of the Soviet Union, allowed Europe's new order, and its new idealism, to blossom fully into a grand plan for world order. Freed from the requirements of any military deterrence, internal or external, Europeans became still more confident that their way of settling international problems now had universal application. Their belief in the importance and relevance of security organizations like NATO diminished by equal measure.

"The genius of the founding fathers," European Commission President Romano Prodi explained, "lay in translating extremely high political ambitions . . . into a series of more specific, almost technical decisions. This indirect approach made further action possible. Rapprochement took place gradually. From confrontation we moved to willingness to cooperate in the economic sphere and then on to integration."[43] This is what many Europeans

[43] Speech by Romano Prodi at the Institut d'Etudes Politiques in Paris, May 29, 2001.

believe they have to offer the world: not power, but the transcendence of power. The "essence" of the European Union, writes Everts, is "all about subjecting inter-state relations to the rule of law," and Europe's experience of successful multilateral governance has, in turn, produced an ambition to convert the world.[44] Europe "has a role to play in world 'governance,' " says Prodi, a role based on replicating the European experience on a global scale. In Europe "the rule of law has replaced the crude interplay of power . . . power politics have lost their influence." And by "making a success of integration we are demonstrating to the world that it is possible to create a method for peace."

No doubt there are Britons, Germans, French, and others who would frown on such exuberant idealism. But many Europeans, including many in positions of power, routinely apply Europe's experience to the rest of the world, and sometimes with the evangelic zeal of converts. The general European critique of the American approach to rogue regimes is based on this special European insight. Iraq, North Korea, Iran, Libya—these states may be dangerous and unpleasant, and even, if simplistic Americans insist, evil. But Germany was evil once, too. Might not an "indirect approach" work again, as it did in Europe? Might it not be possible once more to move from confrontation to rapprochement, beginning with cooperation in the economic sphere and then moving on to peaceful integration? Could not the formula that worked in Europe work again with Iran? Might it have even worked with Iraq? A great many Europeans have insisted that it might, and at less

44 Everts, "Unilateral America, Lightweight Europe?," p. 10.

cost and risk than war. And Europe would apply its lesson to Israelis and Palestinians as well, for, after all, as EU Commissioner Chris Patten argues, "European integration shows that compromise and reconciliation is possible after generations of prejudice, war and suffering."[45] The transmission of the European miracle to the rest of the world has become Europe's new *mission civilisatrice*. Just as Americans have always believed that they had discovered the secret to human happiness and wished to export it to the rest of the world, so Europeans have a new mission born of their own discovery of perpetual peace.

Thus we arrive at what may be the most important reason for the divergence in views between Europe and the United States. America's power and its willingness to exercise that power—unilaterally if necessary—constitute a threat to Europe's new sense of mission. Perhaps it is the greatest threat. American policymakers have found it hard to believe, but leading officials and politicians in Europe really have worried more about how the United States might handle or mishandle the problem of Iraq—by undertaking unilateral and extralegal military action—than they have ever worried about Iraq itself and Saddam Hussein's weapons of mass destruction. And while it is true that they have feared such action might destabilize the Middle East and lead to the unnecessary loss of life, there has always been a deeper concern.[46] Such American

[45] Chris Patten, "From Europe with Support," *Yediot Ahronot,* October 28, 2002.

[46] The common American argument that European policy toward Iraq and Iran has been dictated by financial considerations is only partly right. Are Europeans greedier than Americans? Do American

action, even if successful, is an assault on the essence of "postmodern" Europe. It is an assault on Europe's new ideals, a denial of their universal validity, much as the monarchies of eighteenth- and nineteenth-century Europe were an assault on American republican ideals. Americans ought to be the first to understand that a threat to one's beliefs can be as frightening as a threat to one's physical security.

As Americans have for two centuries, Europeans speak with great confidence of the superiority of their global understanding, the wisdom they have to offer other nations about conflict resolution, and their way of addressing international problems. But just as in the first decade of the American republic, there is a hint of insecurity in the European claim to success, an evident need to have their success affirmed and their views accepted by other nations, particularly by the United States. After all, to deny the validity of the new European idealism is to raise profound doubts about the viability of the European project. If international problems cannot, in fact, be settled the European way, wouldn't that suggest that Europe itself may eventually fall short of a solution, with all the horrors this implies? That is one reason Europeans were so adamant about preserving the universal applicability of the International Criminal Court. For the United States to demand immunity, a double standard for the powerful, is to under-

corporations not influence American policy in Asia and Latin America as well as in the Middle East? The difference is that American strategic judgments sometimes conflict with and override financial interests. For the reasons suggested in this essay, that conflict is much less common for Europeans.

mine the very principle Europeans are trying to establish—
that all nations, strong and weak, are equal under the law
and all must abide by the law. If this principle can be
flouted, even by the benevolent superpower, then what
happens to the European Union, which depends for its very
existence on common obedience to the laws of Europe?
If international law does not reign supreme, is Europe
doomed to return to its past?

And, of course, it is precisely this fear of sliding backward that still hangs over Europeans, even as Europe
moves forward. Europeans, particularly the French and
the Germans, are not entirely sure that the problem once
known as the "German problem" really has been solved.
Neither France under François Mitterrand nor Britain
under Margaret Thatcher was pleased at the prospect of
German reunification after the end of the Cold War; each
had to be coaxed along and reassured by the Americans,
just as British and French leaders had been coaxed along
to accept German reintegration four decades before. As
their various and often very different proposals for the
future constitution of Europe suggest, the French are
still not confident they can trust the Germans, and the
Germans are still not sure they can trust themselves.
Nearly six decades after the end of World War II, a French
official can still remark: "People say, 'It is a terrible thing
that Germany is not working.' But I say, 'Really? When
Germany is working, six months later it is usually march-
ing down the Champs Elysées.' "[47] Buried not very deeply

[47] See Gerard Baker, "Europe's Three Ways of Dealing with Iraq,"
Financial Times, October 17, 2002, p. 17.

beneath the surface of such jokes lies a genuine, lingering trepidation about a Germany that is still too big for the European continent. Last summer, when German Chancellor Gerhard Schroeder defied the Bush administration's call for European support in Iraq, his insistence on dealing with such matters in "the German way" was perhaps even more unsettling to his European neighbors than it was to the United States. Ironically, even German pacifism and neutralism can frighten Europeans when a German leader speaks of "the German way."

Such fears can at times hinder progress toward deeper integration, but they also have driven the European project forward despite innumerable obstacles. European integration is propelled forward in part by the Germans' fears about themselves. The European project must succeed, Joschka Fischer warns, for how else can "the risks and temptations objectively inherent in Germany's dimensions and central situation" be overcome?[48] Those historic German "temptations" play at the back of many a European mind. And every time Europe contemplates the use of military force, or is forced to do so by the United States, there is no avoiding at least momentary consideration of what effect such a military action might have on the "German question" that seems never entirely to disappear.

Perhaps it is not just coincidence, therefore, that the amazing progress toward European integration in recent years has been accompanied not by the emergence of a European superpower but by a diminishing of European

[48] Fischer speech at Humboldt University, May 12, 2000.

military capabilities relative to the United States. Turning Europe into a global superpower capable of balancing the power of the United States may have been one of the original selling points of the European Union—an independent European foreign and defense policy was supposed to be one of the most important by-products of European integration. But, in truth, isn't the ambition for European "power" something of an anachronism? It is an atavistic impulse, inconsistent with the ideals of post-modern Europe, whose very existence depends on the rejection of power politics. Whatever its architects may have intended, European integration has proved to be the enemy of European military power and, indeed, of an important European global role.

This phenomenon has manifested itself not only in flat or declining European defense budgets, but in other ways, too, even in the realm of "soft" power. European leaders talk of Europe's essential role in the world. Prodi yearns "to make our voice heard, to make our actions count."[49] And it is true that Europeans spend a great deal of money on foreign aid—more per capita, they like to point out, than does the United States. Europeans engage in overseas military missions, so long as the missions are mostly limited to peacekeeping. But while the EU periodically dips its fingers into troubled international waters in the Middle East or the Korean Peninsula, the truth is that EU foreign policy is probably the most anemic of all the products of European integration. As one sympathetic observer has noted, few European leaders "are giving it much time or

[49] Prodi speech at the Institut d'Etudes Politiques, May 29, 2001.

energy."[50] EU foreign policy initiatives tend to be short-lived and are rarely backed by sustained agreement on the part of the various European powers. That is one reason they are so easily rebuffed. In the Middle East, where so much European money goes to fund Palestinian and other Arab projects, it is still to the United States that Arabs and Israelis alike look for support, assistance, and a safe resolution of their conflict, not to Europe. All of Europe's great economic power seems not to translate into diplomatic influence, in the Middle East or anywhere else where crises have a military component.[51]

It is obvious, moreover, that issues outside of Europe don't attract nearly as much interest among Europeans as purely European issues do. This has surprised and frustrated Americans on all sides of the political and strategic debate: Recall the profound disappointment of American liberals when Europeans failed to mount an effective protest against Bush's withdrawal from the ABM Treaty. Nor did most Europeans, either among the elites or among the common voters, give the slightest thought to Iraq before the Bush administration threatened to invade it.

This European tendency to look inward is understandable, however, given the enormous and difficult agenda of integration. The enlargement of the European Union to more than two dozen member states, the revision of the common economic and agricultural policies, the question of national sovereignty versus supranational governance,

[50] Charles Grant, "A European View of ESDP," working paper, Centre for European Policy Studies, April 2001.

[51] As Grant observes, "An EU that was less impotent militarily would have more diplomatic clout." Grant, "European Defence," p. 2.

the so-called democracy deficit, the jostling of the large European powers, the dissatisfaction of the smaller powers, the establishment of a new European constitution—all of these present serious and unavoidable challenges. The difficulties of moving forward might seem insuperable were it not for the progress the project of European integration has already demonstrated.

American policies that have been unwelcome in substance—on a missile defense system and the ABM Treaty, belligerence toward Iraq, support for Israel—have been all the more unwelcome because for Europe they are a distraction from the questions that really concern them, namely, questions about Europe. Europeans often point to American insularity and parochialism, but Europeans themselves have turned intensely introspective. As Dominique Moisi has pointed out, last year's French presidential campaign saw "no reference . . . to the events of September 11 and their far-reaching consequences." No one asked, "What should be the role of France and Europe in the new configuration of forces created after September 11? How should France reappraise its military budget and doctrine to take account of the need to maintain some kind of parity between Europe and the United States, or at least between France and the UK?" The Middle East conflict became an issue in the campaign because of France's large Arab and Muslim population, as the high vote for Jean-Marie Le Pen demonstrated. But Le Pen is not a foreign policy hawk. And as Moisi noted, "For most French voters . . . security has little to do with abstract and distant geopolitics. Rather, it is a question of which politician can best protect them from the crime and violence plaguing the streets and suburbs of their cities."[52]

Can Europe change course and assume a larger role on the world stage? There has been no shortage of European leaders urging it to do so. Nor is the weakness of EU foreign policy today necessarily proof that it must be weak tomorrow, given the EU's record of overcoming weaknesses in other areas. And yet the political will to demand more power for Europe appears to be lacking, for the very good reason that Europe does not see a mission for itself that requires power. Its mission, if it has a mission beyond the confines of Europe, is to oppose power. It is revealing that the argument most often advanced by Europeans for augmenting their military strength is not that it will allow Europe to expand its strategic purview or even its global influence. It is merely to rein in and "multilateralize" the United States. "America," writes the pro-American British scholar Timothy Garton Ash, "has too much power for anyone's good, including its own."[53] Therefore Europe must amass power, but for no other reason than to save the world and the United States from the dangers inherent in the present lopsided situation.

Whether that particular mission is a worthy one or not, it seems unlikely to rouse European passions. Only France and Great Britain so far have responded even marginally to this challenge. But France's proposed defense budget increase will prove, like the *force de frappe*, more symbolic than real. Former French foreign minister Hubert

---

[52] Dominique Moisi, *Financial Times*, March 11, 2002.
[53] Timothy Garton Ash, *New York Times*, April 9, 2002.

Védrine, who once complained about American *hyper-puissance*, has stopped talking about counterbalancing the United States. Instead, he shrugs and declares there "is no reason for the Europeans to match a country that can fight four wars at once."[54] It was one thing for Europe in the 1990s to try to increase its annual collective expenditures on defense from $150 billion to $180 billion when the United States was spending $280 billion. But now that the United States is heading toward spending as much as $400 billion per year, or perhaps even more in coming years, Europe has not the slightest intention of keeping up. Thus France might increase its defense budget by 6 percent, prodded by the Gaullism of President Jacques Chirac. The United Kingdom might make an even greater commitment to strengthening and modernizing its military, guided by Tony Blair in an attempt to revive, if on a much smaller scale, an older British tradition of liberal imperialism. But what is "Europe" without Germany? And German defense budgets, today running at about the same percentage of gross domestic product as Luxembourg's, are destined to drop even further in coming years as the German economy struggles under the weight of a stifling labor and social welfare system. European analysts may lament the Continent's "strategic irrelevance." NATO Secretary General George Robertson may call Europe a "military pygmy" in a noble effort to shame Europeans into spending more, and more wisely than they do now. But who honestly believes Europeans will fundamentally change their way of doing business? They have many reasons not to.

[54] Quoted in David Ignatius, "France's Constructive Critic," *Washington Post*, February 22, 2002.

THE WORLD AMERICA MADE

If Americans are unhappy about this state of affairs, they should recall that today's Europe—both the integrated Europe and the weak Europe—is very much the product of American foreign policy stretching back over the better part of nine decades. The United States abandoned Europe after World War I, standing aside as the Continent slipped into a war even more horrible than the first. Even as World War II was ending, the initial American impulse was to walk away again. Franklin Delano Roosevelt's original wartime vision had been to make Europe strategically irrelevant.[55] In the late 1930s and even during the war, the common conviction of Americans was that "the European system was basically rotten, that war was endemic on that continent, and the Europeans had only themselves to blame for their plight."[56] Europe appeared to be nothing more than the overheated incubator of world wars that cost America dearly.

During World War II, Americans like Roosevelt, looking backward rather than forward, believed no greater service could be performed than to take Europe out of the global strategic picture once and for all. Roosevelt actually

[55] As the historian John Lamberton Harper has put it, FDR wanted "to bring about a radical reduction in the weight of Europe" and thereby make possible "the retirement of Europe from world politics." Harper, *American Visions of Europe: Franklin D. Roosevelt, George F. Kennan, and Dean G. Acheson* (Cambridge, UK, 1996), pp. 79, 3.

[56] William L. Langer and S. Everett Gleason, *The Challenge to Isolation, 1937–1940* (New York, 1952), p. 14.

preferred doing business with Stalin's Russia. "After Germany is disarmed," FDR pointedly asked, "what is the reason for France having a big military establishment?" Charles de Gaulle found such questions "disquieting for Europe and for France," as well he might have. Americans of Roosevelt's era held an old American view of Europe as corrupt and decadent, now mingled with a certain contempt for European weakness and dependence. If the European powers were being stripped of their global reach by military and economic weakness following the destruction of World War II, many Americans were only too happy to hurry the process along. As FDR had put it, "When we've won the war, I will work with all my might and main to see to it that the United States is not wheedled into the position of accepting any plan that will further France's imperialistic ambitions, or that will aid or abet the British Empire in its imperial ambitions."[57]

When the Cold War dawned, Americans such as Dean Acheson hoped to create in Europe a powerful partner against the Soviet Union, and most Americans who came of age during the Cold War have always thought of Europe almost exclusively in Achesonian terms—as the essential bulwark of freedom in the struggle against Soviet tyranny. But a suspicious hostility toward Europe always played around the edges of American foreign policy, even during the Cold War. When President Dwight Eisenhower undermined and humiliated Britain and France at Suez in 1956, it was only the most blatant of many American efforts to

[57] Quoted in Selig Adler, *The Isolationist Impulse: Its Twentieth-Century Reaction* (New York, 1957), p. 142; Kissinger, *Diplomacy*, p. 396.

cut Europe down to size and reduce its already weakened global influence.

Nevertheless, for the most part the emerging threat of the Soviet Union compelled Americans to recalculate their relationship with European security, and therefore with the Europeans. And ultimately the more important American contribution to Europe's current world-apart status stemmed not from anti-European but from essentially pro-European impulses. A commitment to Europe, not hostility to it, led the United States in the immediate postwar years to keep troops on the Continent and to create NATO. The presence of American forces as a security guarantee in Europe was, as it was intended to be, the critical ingredient for beginning the process of European integration so that a cohesive "West" would be strong enough materially and spiritually to withstand the daunting challenge of what promised to be a difficult Cold War confrontation with the Soviet Union.

Europe's evolution into its present state occurred under the mantle of the U.S. security guarantee and could not have occurred without it. Not only did the United States for almost half a century supply a shield against such external threats as the Soviet Union and internal threats posed by ethnic conflict in places like the Balkans. More important, the United States was the key to the solution of the "German problem" and perhaps still is. Germany's Fischer, in his Humboldt University speech, noted two "historic decisions" that made the new Europe possible: "the USA's decision to stay in Europe" and "France's and Germany's commitment to the principle of integration, beginning with economic links." But, of course, the latter could never have occurred without the former. France's willingness to risk the reintegration of Germany into Europe—and France was, to say the least, highly dubious—depended on the promise of continued American involvement in Europe as a guarantee against any resurgence of German militarism. Nor were postwar Germans unaware that their own future in Europe depended on the calming presence of the American military.

The current situation abounds in ironies. Europe's rejection of power politics and its devaluing of military force as a tool of international relations have depended on the presence of American military forces on European soil. Europe's new Kantian order could flourish only under the umbrella of American power exercised according to the rules of the old Hobbesian order. American power made it possible for Europeans to believe that power was no longer important. And now, in the final irony, the fact that U.S. military power has solved the European problem, especially the "German problem," allows Europeans today, and Germans in particular, to believe that American military power, and the "strategic culture" that has created and sustained it, is outmoded and dangerous.

Most Europeans do not see or do not wish to see the great paradox: that their passage into post-history has depended on the United States not making the same passage. Because Europe has neither the will nor the ability to guard its own paradise and keep it from being overrun, spiritually as well as physically, by a world that has yet to accept the rule of "moral consciousness," it has become dependent on America's willingness to use its military might to deter or defeat those around the world who still believe in power politics.

Some Europeans do understand the conundrum. Britons, not surprisingly, understand it best. Robert Cooper writes of the need to address the hard truth that although "within the postmodern world [i.e., the Europe of today], there are no security threats in the traditional sense," nevertheless, throughout the rest of the world—what Cooper calls the "modern and pre-modern zones"—threats abound. If the postmodern world does not protect itself, it can be destroyed. But how does Europe protect itself without discarding the very ideals and principles that undergird its pacific system?

"The challenge to the postmodern world," Cooper argues, "is to get used to the idea of double standards." Among themselves, Europeans may "operate on the basis of laws and open cooperative security." But when dealing with the world outside Europe, "we need to revert to the rougher methods of an earlier era—force, preemptive attack, deception, whatever is necessary." This is Cooper's principle for safeguarding society: "Among ourselves, we keep the law, but when we are operating in the jungle, we must also use the laws of the jungle." Cooper directs his argument at Europe, and he couples it with a call for Europeans to cease neglecting their defenses, "both physical and psychological."[58]

Cooper has also served as a close adviser to Tony Blair, and it is clear that Blair, perhaps a good deal more than

[58] Cooper, *The Observer*, April 7, 2002.

his Labour Party followers, has endorsed the idea of an international double standard for power. He has tried to lead Britain into the rule-based Kantian world of the European Union. But as his solidarity with President Bush on the question of Iraq has shown, Blair has also tried to lead Europe back out into the Hobbesian world, where military power remains a key feature of international relations.

But Blair's attempt to bring Europe along with him has been largely unsuccessful. Schroeder has taken his nation "the German way," and France, even under the more conservative Gaullism of Jacques Chirac, has been a most resistant partner of the United States, more intent on constraining American power than in supplementing it with French power.

One suspects that what Cooper has really described, therefore, is not Europe's future but America's present. For it is the United States that has had the difficult task of navigating between these two worlds, trying to abide by, defend, and further the laws of advanced civilized society while simultaneously employing military force against those who refuse to abide by such rules. The United States is already operating according to Cooper's double standard, for the very reasons he suggests. American leaders, too, believe that global security and a liberal order—as well as Europe's "postmodern" paradise—cannot long survive unless the United States does use its power in the dangerous Hobbesian world that still flourishes outside Europe.

What this means is that although the United States has played the critical role in bringing Europe into this Kantian paradise, and still plays a key role in making that para-

dise possible, it cannot enter the paradise itself. It mans
the walls but cannot walk through the gate. The United
States, with all its vast power, remains stuck in history, left
to deal with the Saddams and the ayatollahs, the Kim Jong
Ils and the Jiang Zemins, leaving most of the benefits to
others.

IS IT STILL "THE WEST"?

If this evolving international arrangement continues to
produce a greater American tendency toward unilateralism in international affairs, this should not surprise any
objective observer. In return for manning the walls of
Europe's postmodern order, the United States naturally
seeks a certain freedom of action to deal with the strategic
dangers that it alone has the means and sometimes the
will to address. This is the great problem for relations
between the United States and Europe, of course. For just
at the moment when Europeans, freed of Cold War fears
and constraints, have begun settling into their postmodern paradise and proselytizing for their doctrines of international law and international institutions, Americans
have begun turning in the other direction, away from the
common solidarity with Europe that had been the central
theme of the Cold War and back toward a more traditional American policy of independence, toward that
uniquely American form of universalistic nationalism.

The end of the Cold War had an even more profound
effect on the transatlantic relationship than is commonly

understood, for the common Soviet enemy and the consequent need to act in concert for the common defense were not all that disappeared after 1989. So, too, did a grand strategy pursued on both sides of the Atlantic to preserve and strengthen the cohesion and unity of what was called "the West." It was not just that the United States and Europe had had to work together to meet the Soviet challenge. More than that, the continued unity and success of the liberal Western order was for many years the very definition of victory in the Cold War.

Partly for this reason, American strategy during the Cold War often consisted of providing more to friends and allies than was expected from them in return. To a remarkable degree, American governments measured the success of their foreign policy not by how well the United States was doing by any narrow reckoning of the national interest, but rather by how well America's allies were faring against the many internal and external challenges they faced. Thus it was American economic strategy to raise up from the ruins of World War II powerful economic competitors in Europe and Asia, even to the point where, by the last decades of the Cold War, the United States seemed to many to be in a state of relative decline compared to its increasingly prosperous allies. It was American military strategy to risk nuclear attack upon its otherwise unthreatened homeland in order to deter both nuclear and conventional attacks on European and Asian allies. When one considers the absence of similarly reliable guarantees among the various European powers in the past, between, say, Great Britain and France in the 1920s and

1930s, the willingness of the United States, standing in relative safety behind two oceans, to link its very survival to that of other nations was rather extraordinary.

America's strategic and economic "generosity," if one can call it that, was, of course, closely related to American interests. As Acheson put it, "For the United States to take steps to strengthen countries threatened with Soviet aggression or Communist subversion . . . was to protect the security of the United States—it was to protect freedom itself."[59] But this identification of the interests of others with its own interests was a striking quality of American foreign and defense policy after World War II. After Munich, after Pearl Harbor, and after the onset of the Cold War, Americans increasingly embraced the conviction that their own well-being depended fundamentally on the well-being of others, that American prosperity could not occur in the absence of global prosperity, that American national security was impossible without a broad measure of international security. This was a doctrine of self-interest, but it was the most enlightened kind of self-interest—to the point where it was at times almost indistinguishable from idealism.

Almost, but never entirely. Idealism was never the sole source of American generosity or its propensity to seek to work in concert with its allies. American Cold War multilateralism was more instrumental than idealistic in its motives. After all, "going it alone" after 1945 meant going it alone against the Soviet Union. Going it alone meant shearing apart the West. Nor was it really conceivable,

[59] Quoted in Kissinger, *Diplomacy*, p. 452.

with Soviet troops massed in the heart of Europe, for any American foreign policy to succeed if it was not "multi-lateral" in its inclusion of Western European interests. On the other hand, genuine idealistic multilateralism had been interred for most Americans along with Wilson and the League of Nations Covenant. Dean Acheson, among the leading architects of the postwar international order, considered the UN Charter "impracticable" and the United Nations itself an example of a misguided Wilsonian "faith in the perfectibility of man and the advent of universal peace and law."[60] He and most others present at the creation of the postwar order were idealists, but they were practical idealists. They believed it was essential to present a common Western front to the Communist bloc, and if that meant swallowing what Acheson disparaged as the "holy writ" of the UN Charter, they were prepared to play along. For Acheson, support for the UN was nothing more than "an aid to diplomacy."[61] This is important, because many aspects of American behavior during the Cold War that both Europeans and many Americans in retrospect find so admirable, and whose passing they so lament, represented concessions made in the cause of Western unity.

That unity was not always easy to maintain. American hostility to de Gaulle's determined independence, American suspicion about British imperialism, arguments over Germany's *Ostpolitik,* strategic debates over arms agreements and arms buildups, especially during the Reagan years, all threatened to open cracks in the alliance. But

[60] Quoted in James Chace, *Acheson: The Secretary of State Who Created the American World* (New York, 1998), p. 107.

[61] Ibid., p. 108.

the cracks were always healed, because everyone agreed that while disagreements were inevitable, fissures were dangerous. If "the West" was divided, it would fall. The danger was not only strategic; it was ideological, even psychological. "The West" had to mean something, otherwise what were we defending? And, of course, during the Cold War, "the West" did mean something. It was the liberal, democratic choice of a large segment of humanity, standing in opposition to the alternative choice that existed on the other side of the Berlin Wall.

This powerful strategic, ideological, and psychological need to demonstrate that there was indeed a cohesive, unified West went down with the Berlin Wall and the statues of Lenin in Moscow. The loss was partly masked during the 1990s. Many saw the struggles in Bosnia and Kosovo as a new test of the West. The enlargement of NATO to include former Warsaw Pact nations was an ingathering of peoples who had been forcibly excluded from the West and wanted to be part of it again. They saw NATO as not only or even primarily a security organization but simply as the one and only institution that embodied the transatlantic West. Certainly, the United Nations was not "the West."

But the very success of the transatlantic project, the solution of the European security dilemma, the solution of the German problem, the completion of a Europe "whole and free," the settlement of the Balkan conflicts, the creation of a fairly stable zone of peace and democracy on the European continent—all these great and once unimaginable accomplishments had the inevitable effect of diminishing the significance of "the West." It was not that the West had ceased to exist. Nor was it that the West had ceased to face enemies, for surely militant Muslim fundamentalism is an implacable enemy of the West. But the central point of Francis Fukuyama's famous essay, "The End of History," was irrefutable: The centuries-long struggle among opposing conceptions of how mankind might govern itself had been definitively settled in favor of the Western liberal ideal. Muslim fundamentalism might have its following in the parts of the world where Muslims predominate. Nor can we doubt any longer its capacity to inflict horrific damage on the West. But as Fukuyama and others have pointed out, Muslim fundamentalism does not present a serious challenge to the universal principles of Western liberalism. The existence of Muslim fundamentalism may force Americans and Europeans to defend themselves against devastating attack, and even to cooperate in providing a common defense. But it does not force "the West" to prove itself unified and coherent, as Soviet communism once had.

With less need to preserve and demonstrate the existence of a cohesive "West," it was inevitable that the generosity that had characterized American foreign policy for fifty years would diminish after the Cold War ended. This may be something to lament, but it is not something to be surprised at. The existence of the Soviet Union and the international communist threat had disciplined Americans and made them see that their enlightened self-interest lay in a relatively generous foreign policy, especially toward Europe. After the end of the Cold War, that discipline was no longer present. The end of the Cold War subtly shifted the old equation between idealism and interest. Indeed, those who decry the decline of American generosity in the post–Cold War era must at least reckon with the logic of that decline. Since Americans objectively had less interest in a foreign policy characterized by generosity, for the United States to have maintained the same degree of generosity in its foreign policy as it had during the Cold War, the same commitment to international institutions, the same concern for and deference to allies, the American people would have had to become even more idealistic.

In fact, Americans are no more or less idealistic than they were fifty years ago. It is objective reality that has changed, not the American character. It was the changed international circumstances after the Cold War that opened the way to political forces in Congress, chiefly though not exclusively Republican, which aimed to rewrite old multilateral agreements and defeat new ones, to extricate the United States from treaty obligations now considered onerous or excessively intrusive into American sovereignty. What was new was not the existence of such forces and attitudes, for they had always been present in American politics. They had dominated American politics throughout the 1920s and 1930s, a period ushered in by a Republican president promising a "return to normalcy" after the ambitious idealism of the Wilson years. But during the Cold War, and especially during the years dominated by Republican presidents from Nixon to Reagan, the grand anti-communist strategy had overwhelmed such narrow nationalist sentiments and trumped concerns for sovereignty.

Nor was America's post–Cold War turn toward a more nationalist approach to foreign policy simply the product of a rising Republican Right. Realist international relations theorists and policymakers, the dominant intellectual force in the American foreign policy establishment, also pushed the United States back in the direction of a more narrow nationalism. They decried what Michael Mandelbaum famously called the "international social work" allegedly undertaken by the Clinton administration in Bosnia and Haiti. They insisted that the United States return to a more intent focus on the "national interest," now more narrowly defined than it had been during the Cold War. American realists from Brent Scowcroft to Colin Powell to James Baker to Lawrence Eagleburger did not believe the United States should take on the burden of solving the Balkan crisis or other "humanitarian" crises around the world. The Cold War was over, they argued, and it was therefore possible for American foreign policy to "return to normal."

Post–Cold War "normalcy," however, meant fewer concessions to international public opinion, less deference to allies, more freedom to act as the United States saw fit. These realists gave intellectual legitimacy to the forces in Congress who coupled talk of the "national interest" with calls for reductions in overseas involvements of all kind. If the "national interest" was to be narrowly conceived, many Republicans asked, why, exactly, was it still in the "national interest" for the United States to pay its comparatively exorbitant UN dues? A case that had been easier to make when the preservation of Western unity against communism was the goal of American foreign policy was now harder to make in the absence of such a far-reaching and enlightened definition of the American "national interest."

Even the Clinton administration, more idealistic and, perhaps ironically, more wedded to the Cold War foreign policy of generosity than the realists and Republicans, nevertheless could not escape the new post–Cold War reality. It was Clinton, after all, who ran for president in 1992 on a platform declaring that the American economy mattered and foreign policy did not. Clinton stepped in to try to repair "the West" only after trying desperately not to take on that responsibility. When the administration of George W. Bush came to office in January 2001, bringing with it the realist-nationalism of 1990s Republicanism, "the West" as a functioning concept in American foreign policy had become dormant. When the terrorists struck the United States eight months later, the Cold War equation was completely inverted. Now, with the threat brought directly to American soil, overleaping that of America's allies, the paramount issue was America's unique suffering and vulnerability, not "the West."

The declining significance of "the West" as an organizing principle of foreign policy was not just an American phenomenon, however. Post–Cold War Europe agreed that the issue was no longer "the West." For Europeans, the issue became "Europe." Proving that there was a united Europe took precedence over proving that there was a united West. A European "nationalism" mirrored the American nationalism, and although this was not Europe's intent, the present gap between the United States and Europe today may be traced in part to Europe's decision to establish itself as a single entity apart from the United States.

This effort impressed on American minds that the

transatlantic goal was no longer a unified West; the Europeans themselves no longer thought in such terms. Instead, Europeans spoke of "Europe" as another pole in a new multipolar world—a counterbalance to America. Europe would establish its own separate foreign policy and defense "identity" outside of NATO. The institutions Europeans revered were the European Union and the United Nations. But for Americans, as for Central and Eastern Europeans, the UN was not "the West," and the European Union was not "the West." Only NATO was "the West," and now Europeans were building an alternative to NATO. Everything the Europeans were doing made sense from a European perspective; and the project of European integration was objectively of benefit to the United States, at least insofar as it strengthened the peace. Nor was it the intention of most Europeans to raise a challenge to the United States, much less to the idea of "the West." But how surprising was it that Americans no longer placed as high a priority on the unity of the West and the cohesion of the alliance as they once had? Europeans had undertaken an all-consuming project in which the United States by definition could have no part. The United States, meanwhile, has projects of its own.

ADJUSTING TO HEGEMONY

America did not change on September 11. It only became more itself. Nor should there be any mystery about the course America is on, and has been on, not only over the past year or over the past decade, but for the better part of the past six decades, and, one might even say, for the better part of the past four centuries. It is an objective fact that Americans have been expanding their power and influence in ever-widening arcs since even before they founded their own independent nation. The hegemony that America established within the Western Hemisphere in the nineteenth century has been a permanent feature of international politics ever since. The expansion of America's strategic reach into Europe and East Asia that came with the Second World War has never been retracted. Indeed, it is somewhat remarkable to reflect that more than fifty years after the end of that war—a period that has seen Japanese and German enemies completely transformed into valued friends and allies—and more than a decade after the Cold War—which ended in another stunning transformation of a defeated foe—the United States nevertheless remains, and clearly intends to remain, the dominant strategic force in both East Asia and Europe. The end of the Cold War was taken by Americans as an opportunity not to retract but to expand their reach, to expand the alliance they lead eastward toward Russia, to strengthen their relations among the increasingly democratic powers of East Asia, to stake out interests in parts of the world, like Central Asia, that most Americans never knew existed before.

The myth of America's "isolationist" tradition is remarkably resilient. But it is a myth. Expansion of territory and influence has been the inescapable reality of American history, and it has not been an unconscious expansion. The ambition to play a grand role on the world stage is deeply rooted in the American character. Since independence and even before, Americans who disagreed on many things always shared a common belief in their nation's great destiny. Even as a weak collection of loosely united colonies stretched out across the Atlantic Coast, threatened on all sides by European empires and an untamed wilderness, the United States had appeared to its leaders a "Hercules in the cradle," "the embryo of a great empire." To the generation of the early republic, to Washington, Hamilton, Franklin, and Jefferson, nothing was more certain than that the North American continent would be subdued, American wealth and population would grow, and the young republic would someday come to dominate the Western Hemisphere and take its place among the world's great powers. Jefferson foresaw the establishment of a vast "empire of liberty." Hamilton believed America would, "erelong, assume an attitude correspondent with its great destinies—majestic, efficient, and operative of great things. A noble career lies before it."[62]

For those early generations of Americans, the promise of national greatness was not merely a comforting hope but an integral part of the national identity, inextricably entwined with the national ideology. The United States must become a great power, and perhaps the greatest power, they and many subsequent generations of Americans believed, because the principles and ideals upon which it was founded were unquestionably superior— superior not only to those of the corrupt monarchies of eighteenth- and nineteenth-century Europe, but to the ideas that had shaped nations and governments through-

[62] Quoted in Stourzh, *Alexander Hamilton*, p. 195.

out human history. The proof of the transcendent importance of the American experiment would be found not only in the continual perfection of American institutions at home but also in the spread of American influence in the world. Americans have always been internationalists, therefore, but their internationalism has always been a by-product of their nationalism. When Americans sought legitimacy for their actions abroad, they sought it not from supranational institutions but from their own principles. That is why it was always so easy for so many Americans to believe, as so many still believe today, that by advancing their own interests they advance the interests of humanity. As Benjamin Franklin put it, America's "cause is the cause of all mankind."[63]

This enduring American view of their nation's exceptional place in history, their conviction that their interests and the world's interests are one, may be welcomed, ridiculed, or lamented. But it should not be doubted. And just as there is little reason to expect Europe to change its fundamental course, there is little cause to believe the United States will change its own course, or begin to conduct itself in the world in a fundamentally different manner. Absent some unforeseen catastrophe—not a setback in Iraq or "another Vietnam," but a military or economic calamity great enough to destroy the very sources of American power—it is reasonable to assume that we have only just entered a long era of American hegemony. Demographic trends show the American population growing

[63] Quoted in Edward Handler, *America and Europe in the Political Thought of John Adams* (Cambridge, MA, 1964), p. 102.

faster and getting younger while the European population declines and steadily ages. According to *The Economist*, if present trends continue, the American economy, now roughly the same size as the European economy, could grow to be more than twice the size of Europe's by 2050. Today the median age of Americans is 35.5; in Europe it is 37.7. By 2050, the American median age will be 36.2. In Europe, if present trends persist, it will be 52.7. That means, among other things, that the financial burden of caring for elderly dependents will grow much higher in Europe than in the United States. And that means Europeans will have even less money to spend on defense in the coming years and decades than they do today. As *The Economist* observes, "The long-term logic of demography seems likely to entrench America's power and to widen existing transatlantic rifts," providing a stark "contrast between youthful, exuberant, multi-coloured America and ageing, decrepit, inward-looking Europe."[64]

If America's relative power will not diminish, neither are Americans likely to change their views of how that power is to be used. In fact, despite all the seismic geopolitical shifts that have occurred since 1941, Americans have been fairly consistent in their thinking about the nature of world affairs and about America's role in shaping the world to suit its interests and ideals. The founding document of the Cold War, Kennan's "Long Telegram," starkly set out the dominant perspective of America's postwar strategic culture: The Soviet Union was "impervious to the logic of reason," Kennan wrote, but would

[64] "Half a Billion Americans?," *The Economist,* August 22, 2002.

be "highly sensitive to the logic of force."[65] A good liberal Democrat like Clark Clifford agreed that the "language of military power" was the only language that the Soviets understood, and that the Soviet empire had to be considered a "distinct entity with which conflict is not predestined but with which we cannot pursue common goals."[66] Few Americans would put things that starkly today, but many Americans would agree with the sentiments. Last year large majorities of Democrats and Republicans in both houses of Congress agreed that the "language of military power" might be all that Saddam Hussein understood.

It is not that Americans never flirted with the kind of internationalist idealism that now permeates Europe. In the first half of the twentieth century, Americans fought Wilson's "war to end all wars," which was followed a decade later by an American secretary of state putting his signature to a treaty outlawing war. In the 1930s, Franklin Roosevelt put his faith in nonaggression pacts and asked merely that Hitler promise not to attack a list of countries Roosevelt presented to him. Even after the Yalta conference of 1945, a dying FDR could proclaim "the end of the system of unilateral action, the exclusive alliances, the spheres of influence, the balances of power," and to promise in their stead "a universal organization in which all peace-loving Nations will finally have a chance to join . . . a permanent structure of peace."[67] But Roosevelt no

[65] Quoted in Chace, *Acheson*, p. 150.
[66] Quoted in ibid., p. 157.
[67] Quoted in Kissinger, *Diplomacy*, p. 416.

longer had full confidence in such a possibility. After Munich and Pearl Harbor, and then, after a fleeting moment of renewed idealism, the plunge into the Cold War, Kennan's "logic of force" became the operating assumption of American strategy. Acheson spoke of building up "situations of strength" around the globe. The "lesson of Munich" came to dominate American strategic thought, and although it was supplanted for a brief time by the "lesson of Vietnam," today it remains the dominant paradigm. While a small segment of the American elite still yearns for "global governance" and eschews military force, Americans from Madeleine Albright to Donald Rumsfeld, from Brent Scowcroft to Anthony Lake, still remember Munich, figuratively if not literally. And for younger generations of Americans who do not remember Munich or Pearl Harbor, there is now September 11. One of the things that most clearly divides Europeans and Americans today is a philosophical, even metaphysical disagreement over where exactly mankind stands on the continuum between the laws of the jungle and the laws of reason. Americans do not believe we are as close to the realization of the Kantian dream as do Europeans.

So where do we go from here? Again, it is not hard to see where America is going. The September 11 attacks shifted and accelerated but did not fundamentally alter a course the United States was already on. They certainly did not alter but only reinforced American attitudes toward power. Recall that even before September 11, Acheson's successors were still, if somewhat distractedly, building "situations of strength" around the world. Before September 11, and indeed, even before the election of George

W. Bush, American strategic thinkers and Pentagon plan-
ners were looking ahead to the next strategic challenges
that seemed likely to arise. One of those challenges was
Iraq. During the Clinton years, Congress had passed by a
nearly unanimous vote a bill authorizing military and
financial support for Iraqi opposition forces, and the second Bush administration was considering plans to destabilize Iraq before the terrorists struck on September 11.
The Clinton administration also laid the foundations for
a new ballistic missile defense system to defend against
rogue states such as Iraq, Iran, and North Korea. Had Al
Gore been elected, and had there been no terrorist attacks
on September 11, these programs—aimed squarely at
Bush's "axis of evil"—would still be under way.

Americans before September 11 were augmenting, not
diminishing, their military power. In the 2000 election
campaign, Bush and Gore both promised to increase
defense spending, responding not to any particular threat
but only to the general perception that the American
defense budget—then running at close to $300 billion
per year—was inadequate to meet the nation's strategic
requirements. American military and civilian leaders inside
and outside the Pentagon were seized with the need to
modernize American forces, to take advantage of what
was and is regarded as a "revolution in military affairs"
that could change the very nature of the way wars are
fought. Behind this enthusiasm was a genuine concern
that if the United States did not make the necessary invest-
ments in technological transformation, its forces, its security, and the world's security would be at risk in the future.

Before September 11, the American strategic community had begun to focus its attention on China. Few believed that a war with China was probable in the near future—unless as a result of some crisis over Taiwan—but many believed that some confrontation with China would become increasingly likely within the coming two decades, as China's military capacity and geopolitical ambitions grew. This concern about China was one of the driving forces behind the demand for technological modernization of the American military; it was, quietly, one of the motives behind the push for a new missile defense program; and in a broad sense it had already become an organizing principle of American strategic planning. The view of China as the next big strategic challenge took hold in the Clinton Pentagon, and was given official sanction by President Bush when he declared pointedly before and after his election that China was not a strategic partner but a strategic competitor of the United States.

When the Bush administration released its new National Security Strategy in September of last year, the ambitiousness of American strategy left many Europeans, and even some Americans, breathless. The new strategy was seen as a response to September 11, and perhaps in the minds of those who wrote it, it was. But the striking thing about that document is that aside from a few references to the idea of "pre-emption," which itself was hardly a novel concept, the Bush administration's "new" strategy was little more than a restatement of American policies, many going back a half century. The Bush strategy said nothing about the promotion of democracy abroad that had not been said with at least equal fervor by Harry Truman, John F. Kennedy, or Ronald Reagan. The declaration of

America's intent to remain the world's pre-eminent military power, and to remain strong enough to discourage any other power from challenging American pre-eminence, was merely the public expression of what had been an unspoken premise of American strategic planning—if not of actual defense spending and military capability—since the end of the Cold War.

The policies of the Clinton and Bush administrations, well or ill designed, nevertheless rested on a common and distinctly American assumption—that is, the United States as the "indispensable nation." Americans seek to defend and advance a liberal international order. But the only stable and successful international order Americans can imagine is one that has the United States at its center. Nor can Americans conceive of an international order that is not defended by power, and specifically by American power. If this is arrogance, at least it is not a new arrogance. Henry Kissinger once asked the aging Harry Truman what he wanted to be remembered for. Truman answered: "We completely defeated our enemies and made them surrender. And then we helped them to recover, to become democratic, and to rejoin the community of nations. Only America could have done that."[68] Even the most hardheaded American realists have grown sentimental contemplating what Reinhold Niebuhr once called America's "responsibility" for "solving . . . the world problem." George Kennan, setting forth his doctrine of containment—which he foresaw would be a terribly difficult strategy for a democracy to sustain—nevertheless saw

[68] Quoted in Kissinger, *Diplomacy*, p. 425.

the challenge as "a test of the overall worth of the United States as a nation among nations." He even suggested that Americans should express their "gratitude to a Providence which, by providing [them] with this implacable challenge, has made their entire security as a nation dependent on their pulling themselves together and accepting the responsibilities of moral and political leadership that history plainly intended them to bear."[69]

Americans are idealists. In some matters, they may be more idealistic than Europeans. But they have no experience of promoting ideals successfully without power. Certainly, they have no experience of successful supranational governance; little to make them place all their faith in international law and international institutions, much as they might wish to; and even less to let them travel, with the Europeans, beyond power. Americans, as good children of the Enlightenment, still believe in the perfectibility of man, and they retain hope for the perfectibility of the world. But they remain realists in the limited sense that they still believe in the necessity of power in a world that remains far from perfection. Such law as there may be to regulate international behavior, they believe, exists because a power like the United States defends it by force of arms. In other words, just as Europeans claim, Americans can still sometimes see themselves in heroic terms—as Gary Cooper at high noon. They will defend the townspeople, whether the townspeople want them to or not.

Today, as a result of the September 11 terrorist attacks,

[69] X [George F. Kennan], "The Sources of Soviet Conduct," p. 169.

the United States is embarked on yet another expansion of its strategic purview. Just as the Japanese attack on Pearl Harbor, which should not really have come as such a surprise, led to an enduring American role in East Asia and in Europe, so September 11, which future historians will no doubt depict as the inevitable consequence of American involvement in the Muslim world, will likely produce a lasting American military presence in the Persian Gulf and Central Asia, and perhaps a long-term occupation of one of the Arab world's largest countries. Americans may be surprised to find themselves in such a position, just as Americans of the 1930s would have been stunned to find themselves an occupying power in both Germany and Japan less than a decade later. But viewed from the perspective of the grand sweep of American history, a history marked by the nation's steady expansion and a seemingly ineluctable rise from perilous weakness to the present global hegemony, this latest expansion of America's strategic role may be less than shocking.

What does all this mean for the transatlantic relationship? Can Europe possibly follow where America leads? And if it cannot, does that matter?

One answer to these questions is that the crisis over Iraq has cast the transatlantic problem in the harshest possible light. When that crisis subsides, as in time it will, the questions of power that most divide Americans and Europeans may subside a bit as well; the common political culture and the economic ties that bind Americans and Europeans will then come to the fore—until the next international strategic crisis. But perhaps the next crisis will not bring out transatlantic disagreements as severely as the crisis over Iraq and the greater Middle East—a region where both American and European interests are great but where American and European differences have proved especially acute. The next international crisis could come in East Asia. Given its distance from Europe and the smaller European interest there, and the fact that Europeans could bring even less power to bear in East Asia than they can in the Middle East, thereby making them even less relevant to American strategic planning, it is possible that an Asian crisis would not lead to another transatlantic divide of the magnitude of that which we have been experiencing.

In short, although it is difficult to foresee a closing of the gap between American and European perceptions of the world, that gap may be more manageable than it currently appears. There need be no "clash of civilizations" within what used to be called "the West." The task, for both Europeans and Americans, is to readjust to the new reality of American hegemony. And perhaps, as the psychiatrists like to claim, the first step in managing this problem is to understand it and to acknowledge that it exists.

Certainly Americans, when they think about Europe, should not lose sight of the main point: The new Europe is indeed a blessed miracle and a reason for enormous celebration—on both sides of the Atlantic. For Europeans, it is the realization of a long and improbable dream: a continent free from nationalist strife and blood feuds, from military competition and arms races. War between the major European powers is almost unimaginable. After centuries of misery, not only for Europeans but also for those pulled into their conflicts—as Americans were twice in the past century—the new Europe really has emerged as a paradise. It is something to be cherished and guarded, not least by Americans, who have shed blood on Europe's soil and would shed more should the new Europe ever fail. This does not mean, however, that the United States can or should rely on Europe in the future as it has in the past. Americans should not let nostalgia for what may have been the unusual circumstances of the Cold War mislead them about the nature of their strategic relationship with the European powers in the post–Cold War era.

Can the United States prepare for and respond to the strategic challenges around the world without much help from Europe? The simple answer is that it already does. The United States has maintained strategic stability in Asia with no help from Europe. In the various crises in the Middle East and Persian Gulf over the past decade, including the present one, European help, even when enthusiastically offered, has been token. Whatever Europe can or cannot offer in terms of moral and political support, it has had little to offer the United States in strategic military terms since the end of the Cold War—except, of course, that most valuable of strategic assets, a Europe at peace.

Today the United States spends a little more than 3 percent of its GDP on defense. Were Americans to increase that to 4 percent—meaning a defense budget in excess of $500 billion per year—it would still represent a smaller percentage of national wealth than Americans spent on defense throughout most of the past half century. Even Paul Kennedy, who invented the term "imperial overstretch" in the late 1980s (when the United States was spending around 7 percent of its GDP on defense), believes the United States can sustain its current military spending levels and its current global dominance far into the future. The United States can manage, therefore, at least in material terms. Nor can one argue that the American people are unwilling to shoulder this global burden, since they have done so for a decade already, and after September 11 they seem willing to continue doing so for a long time to come. Americans apparently feel no resentment at not being able to enter Europe's "postmodern" world. There is no evidence that most Americans desire to. Partly because they are so powerful, they take pride in their nation's military power and their nation's special role in the world.

The dangers of the present transatlantic predicament, then, lie neither in American will nor capability, but in the inherent moral tension of the current international situation. As is so often the case in human affairs, the real question is one of intangibles—of fears, passions, and beliefs. The problem is that the United States must sometimes play by the rules of a Hobbesian world, even though in doing so it violates Europe's postmodern norms. It must refuse to abide by certain international conventions that may constrain its ability to fight effectively in Robert Cooper's jungle. It must support arms control, but not always for itself. It must live by a double standard. And it must sometimes act unilaterally, not out of a passion for unilateralism but only because, given a weak Europe that has moved beyond power, the United States has no choice *but* to act unilaterally.

Few Europeans admit, as Cooper does implicitly, that such American behavior may redound to the greater benefit of the civilized world, that American power, even employed under a double standard, may be the best means of advancing human progress—and perhaps the only means. As Niebuhr wrote a half century ago, America's "inordinate power," for all its "perils," provides "some real advantages for the world community."[70] Instead, many Europeans today have come to consider the United States itself to be the outlaw, a rogue colossus. The danger—if it is a danger—is that the United States and Europe could become positively estranged. Europeans could become more and more shrill in their attacks on the United States. The United States could become less inclined to listen, or perhaps even to care. The day could come, if it has not already, when Americans might no more heed the pronouncements of the EU than they do the pronouncements of ASEAN or the Andean Pact.

To those of us who came of age in the Cold War, the strategic decoupling of Europe and the United States seems frightening. De Gaulle, when confronted by FDR's vision of a world where Europe was irrelevant, recoiled and suggested that this vision "risked endangering the Western world." If Western Europe was to be considered a "secondary matter" by the United States, would not FDR only "weaken the very cause he meant to serve—that of civilization?" Western Europe, de Gaulle maintained, was "essential to the West. Nothing can replace the value, the power, the shining example of the ancient peoples." Typically, he insisted this was "true of France above all."[71]

[70] Reinhold Niebuhr, *The Irony of American History* (New York, 1962), p. 134

[71] Quoted in Harper, *American Visions of Europe,* pp. 114-15.

But leaving aside French *amour propre*, did not de Gaulle have a point? If Americans were to decide that Europe was no more than an irritating irrelevancy, would American society gradually become unmoored from what we now call "the West"? It is not a risk to be taken lightly, on either side of the Atlantic.

So what is to be done? The obvious answer is that Europe should follow the course that Cooper, Ash, Robertson, and others recommend and build up its military capabilities, even if only marginally. There is not much ground for hope that this will happen. But, then, who knows? Maybe concern about America's overweening power really will create some energy in Europe. Perhaps the atavistic impulses that still swirl in the hearts of Germans, Britons, and Frenchmen—the memory of power, international influence, and national ambition—can still be played upon. Some Britons still remember empire; some Frenchmen still yearn for *la gloire;* some Germans still want their place in the sun. These urges are now mostly channeled into the grand European project, but they could find more traditional expression. Whether this is to be hoped for or feared is another question. It would be better still if Europeans could move beyond fear and anger at the rogue colossus and remember, again, the vital necessity of having a strong, even predominant America— for the world and especially for Europe. It would seem to be an acceptable price to pay for paradise.

Americans can help. It is true that the Bush administration came into office with something of a chip on its shoulder. The realist-nationalist impulses it inherited from the Republican Congress of the 1990s made it appear almost eager to scorn the opinions of much of the rest of the world. The picture it painted in its early months was of a behemoth thrashing about against constraints that only it could see. It was hostile to the new Europe—as to a lesser extent was the Clinton administration—seeing it not so much as an ally but as an albatross. Even after September 11, when the Europeans offered their very limited military capabilities in the fight in Afghanistan, the United States resisted, fearing that European cooperation was a ruse to tie America down. The Bush administration viewed NATO's historic decision to aid the United States under Article 5 less as a boon than as a booby trap. An opportunity to draw Europe into common battle out in the Hobbesian world, even in a minor role, was thereby unnecessarily squandered.

But Americans are powerful enough that they need not fear Europeans, even when bearing gifts. Rather than viewing the United States as a Gulliver tied down by Lilliputian threads, American leaders should realize that they are hardly constrained at all, that Europe is not really capable of constraining the United States. If the United States could move past the anxiety engendered by this inaccurate sense of constraint, it could begin to show more understanding for the sensibilities of others, a little more of the generosity of spirit that characterized American foreign policy during the Cold War. It could pay its respects to multilateralism and the rule of law, and try to build some international political capital for those moments when multilateralism is impossible and unilateral action unavoidable. It could, in short, take more care to show what the founders called a "decent respect for the opinion of mankind." This was always the wisest policy. And there is certainly benefit in it for the United States: Winning the material and moral support of friends and allies, especially in Europe, is unquestionably preferable to acting alone in the face of European anxiety and hostility.

These are small steps, and they will not address the deep problems that beset the transatlantic relationship today. But, after all, it is more than a cliché that the United States and Europe share a set of common Western beliefs. Their aspirations for humanity are much the same, even if their vast disparity of power has now put them in very different places. Perhaps it is not too naïvely optimistic to believe that a little common understanding could still go a long way.

A NOTE ABOUT THE AUTHOR

Robert Kagan is senior associate at the Carnegie Endowment for International Peace, where he is director of the U.S. Leadership Project. In addition to a monthly column in the *Washington Post,* he is the author of *A Twilight Struggle: American Power and Nicaragua, 1977–1990,* and coeditor, with William Kristol, of *Present Dangers: Crisis and Opportunity in American Foreign and Defense Policy.* Kagan served in the State Department from 1984 to 1988.

A NOTE ON THE TYPE

This book was set in Minion, a typeface produced by the Adobe Corporation specifically for the Macintosh personal computer and released in 1990. Designed by Robert Slimbach, Minion combines the classic characteristics of old-style faces with the full complement of weights required for modern typesetting.